# HOW TO WALK WITH
# GOD
# IN
# GOOD TIMES AND BAD

**DIANE PACHECO**

Copyright © 2023 Diane Pacheco.

All rights reserved. No part of this book may be reproduced, stored, or transmitted by any means—whether auditory, graphic, mechanical, or electronic—without written permission of both publisher and author, except in the case of brief excerpts used in critical articles and reviews. Unauthorized reproduction of any part of this work is illegal and is punishable by law.

ISBN: 979-8-88640-815-7 (sc)
ISBN: 979-8-88640-816-4 (hc)
ISBN: 979-8-88640-817-1 (e)

Because of the dynamic nature of the Internet, any web addresses or links contained in this book may have changed since publication and may no longer be valid. The views expressed in this work are solely those of the author and do not necessarily reflect the views of the publisher, and the publisher hereby disclaims any responsibility for them.

One Galleria Blvd., Suite 1900, Metairie, LA 70001
1-888-421-2397

# TABLE OF CONTENTS

Chapter 1: Faith/Believing ..................................................1

Chapter 2: Trusting God ....................................................21

Chapter 3: Forgiveness ......................................................34

Chapter 4: Trusting God And His Word ...........................48

Chapter 5: Walking with God ...........................................58

Chapter 6: Peace ................................................................66

Chapter 7: Joy ....................................................................74

Chapter 8: God In Christ In Us Through The Holy Spirit ............89

Conclusion ........................................................................107

# CHAPTER 1

## Faith/Believing

We have Faith through our Lord Jesus Christ! We start by believing that Jesus Christ Died and Rose Again to forgive our sins and save us.

> ROMANS 10: 9-13
>
> That if thou shalt confess with thy <u>mouth</u> the Lord Jesus and shalt believe in thine <u>Heart</u> that God hath raised Him from the dead, thou shalt be saved.
>
> For with thine <u>heart</u> man believeth unto righteousness and with the <u>mouth</u> confession is made unto salvation.
>
> For the <u>scripture</u> saith whosoever <u>believeth</u> on <u>Him (Jesus Christ)</u> shall not be ashamed.
>
> For there is no difference between the Jew and the Greek (Gentiles) for the same Lord over all is rich unto all that call upon Him.
>
> For whosoever calleth upon the name of the Lord shall be saved.

God through Jesus Christ and His grace and mercy loves us. Through Faith (believing) we know and thank God and believe He (Jesus Christ) died for us and God raised Him from the dead and now has made available to us all Jesus died for us to have. Because we believe and have knowledge through the word of God, we can enjoy our lives. We can enjoy an amazing walk with God in confidence, peaceful and powerful day by day. Why? Because we trust God in every area of our lives.

MATTHEW 6:30 – 33

Wherefore if God so clothed the grass of the field, which today is and tomorrow is cast into the oven, He shall not much more clothe you, O ye of little faith?

Therefore take no thought saying, What shall we eat or what shall we drink or what withal shall we be clothed?

For after all these things do the Gentiles seek: For your heavenly Father knoweth that ye have need of all these things.

But seek ye First the kingdom of God and His righteousness and all these things shall be added unto you.

God wants to bless us with all we need in the spiritual realm and in what we need. People do not understand their purpose in this life. They give 10 million thoughts on the subject, but if they knew God and His word they would know. Most do not realize or believe their true purpose is to walk with God and serve Him and His will and purpose. Even many mature believers still do not understand this fact. Those who are spiritually mature walking in daily fellowship in His presence and His will and purpose understand what that truly means. Having power through walking in peace, with praise and thanksgiving to God through Jesus Christ through the Holy Spirit, who leads us daily.

JOHN 14:6

Jesus saith unto him, I am the way, the truth and the life, no man cometh unto the Father, but by me.

Jesus died for us to walk in the love of God and has made so much available to us and left us God's word so we can learn what is available to each of us.

JOHN 14: 12 – 17

Verily, verily I say unto you, He that believeth on Me the works that I do shall he do also and greater works than these shall he do because I go unto my Father.

And whatsoever ye shall ask in my name, that will I do that the Father may be glorified in the Son.

And if ye shall ask anything in My name, I will do it.

And I will pray the Father and He shall give you another Comforter (the Holy Spirit) that He may abide with you forever.

Even the Spirit of truth whom the world cannot receive because it seeth Him not, neither knoweth Him, but ye Know Him for He dwelleth with you and shall be in you.

God will help you learn and grow in His love if you ask Him. Learn to ask for the best things available, such as all the spiritual blessings in/from the heavenly realm. There is much we can learn by spending daily time in God's word and talking with Him throughout our day. I like to call my walk with God, "God in Christ through the Holy Spirit in me". Being filled with all that Jesus Christ died for us to have. All the spiritual blessings in the heavenly's. There is so much Jesus Christ left us, so believe in Him and receive what He wants us to have. If you know God and His love it is easy. The Bible, God's word is our number one reference and resource to learn and know God. Ask God to help you through the Holy Spirit and lead you in your walk with Him daily. Spend time in God's word and learn of Him and all that is available to you, including peace and joy and the power of Jesus Christ. I will leave you with a few scriptures you can look at to help you see what is available to you.

Some of what is available to us in this day and time:

| | |
|---|---|
| ACTS 2:38-39 | THE GIFT OF THE HOLY SPIRIT |
| ACTS 10:45 | |
| ROMANS 5:17 | THE FREE GIFT OF GRACE AND RIGHTEOUSNESS |
| EPHESIANS 2:5-10 | THE FREE GIFT OF GRACE |
| 1 CORINTHIANS 12:8 | SPIRIT OF WISDOM AND KNOWLEDGE |

Believing and studying God's word helps us to help others. That is why we are here and what we are called to do. We are called to be a blessing to others and represent our Holy Father on this earth.

> John 13: 34-35
>
> A new commandment I give unto you, That ye love one another; as I have loved you, that ye also love one another.

Jesus stated that after the last supper. That being one of the last things He said to the disciples, I believe it is quite important. Think and ponder that. God has given us His free gift of Grace and we should walk in God's grace and share it with one another.

> Ephesians 2:4-7
>
> But God, who is Rich in Mercy for His Great Love where with He Loved us,
>
> Even when we were dead in sins, hath quickened us together with Christ, (by Grace ye are Saved;)
>
> And hath raised us up together and made us sit together in heavenly places IN Christ:
>
> That in the ages to come He might show the exceeding riches of His grace in Kindness toward US through Christ.

The Key to walking and enjoying PEACE is Believing. Faith and Trust in God in Christ through the Holy Spirit in US. And this is all ours because we Believe in Him with our Heart and Soul and Mind.

Faith = Believing

Believing = Faith

We all have been given faith through Jesus Christ, but we need to use it. Believe and trust God. Walk and talk with Him in everything throughout your day.

> ROMANS 12:6
>
> Having then gifts differing according to the grace that is given to us, whether prophecy, let us prophecy, according to the proportion of Faith (Believing).

We all have Faith and have to use it and apply it in practical application in our lives. Let God know you want to be what He wants you to be and you know He is the only way you can change through the leadership of the Holy Spirit. He will work with you day by day and do a good work in you.

> 2 Corinthians 4:13
>
> We having the same spirit of faith (believing), according as it is written, I believed and therefore have I spoken, we to believe and therefore speak.

We need to practice and develop our faith (believing) through studying and knowing what God's word teaches us. We spend time in the word of God and as believers this is our responsibility in getting to know who we are in Christ. We are told in the word of God to study it.

> 2 Timothy 2:15
>
> Study to shew thyself approved unto God, a workman that needeth not to be ashamed, rightly dividing the word of truth.
>
> 1 Thessalonians 4:11
>
> And that ye study to be quite and to do your own business and to work with your own hands, as we commanded you.
>
> These were more noble than those in Thessalonica, in that they received the word with all readiness of mind and <u>searched</u> the scriptures Daily, whether those things were so.

Truly, if you are not studying and researching the word to develop your faith and trust in God, this may be difficult to understand. You need to do your part and God will do His. I have been studying and researching the word of God for about 30 or so years and spend time in God's word daily. I study the word and other books or commentaries about God's word. If you are having difficulty understanding God's word, there are many other resources and information out there to help you. Today we have so much information available to us right at our finger- tips.

God will help you in all your endeavors to learn and grow in the faith of Jesus Christ. God still shows and teaches me new things as I study and search His word daily as I endeavor to have a close personal relationship with Him. Honestly, my joy and peace come from believing and living the word of God.

> Romans 15:13
>
> Now the God of hope fill you with all joy and peace in believing, that ye may abound in hope, through the Power of the Holy Spirit.

Believing is our key for opening doors that no one else can open and closing doors no one else can close. (Revelation 3:7) The more we believe and search the scriptures, the more God teaches us and helps us in our walk with Him. He knows our hearts and sincerity and commitment to grow in Him. God searches our hearts and knows us well.

> JEREMIAH 17:10
>
> I the Lord search the heart, I try the reins, even to give every man according to his ways and according to the fruit of his doings.

God knows our hearts and motives for what we do and why and He sees if there is any fruit as we walk as His examples. But we need to walk with Him in everything.

> John 6:28-29
>
> Then said they unto Him, what shall we do, that we might work the works of God?

Jesus answered and said unto them, This is the work of God, that ye believe on Him (Jesus) whom He (GOD) hath sent.

Jesus is telling us to Believe in Him and all God has accomplished for us through His blood. The only way to grow in our believing in God, in Christ through the Holy Spirit in us, is to learn and study God's word. Continue growing and seeking God's presence in our lives and letting God work in us as we walk with Him. God works to us and then through us to be a blessing to others. The more we do that the more we grow and the more God Blesses us. This includes those who have hurt us or offended us because then and only then do you really walk with God. That is the perfect strategy for walking in Peace and being blessed. Pray and ask God to help you forgive them and do good unto them walking in the peace of Jesus Christ.

John 14:27

Jesus said, Peace I leave with you, My peace I give unto you, not as the world giveth, give I unto you, Let not your heart be troubled, neither let it be afraid.

Knowing we are walking in confidence in God through Jesus Christ is walking in peace. Behaving the way we know He wants us to and doing good unto others is His will for us. Trusting God and doing good unto others is where we get our peace from.

Peace = Power

To be stable in all the ups and downs in life enables us to continue growing in the knowledge of Him.

HEBREWS 11:6                    – REMEMBER –

But without Faith it is impossible to please Him; for he, that cometh to God must Believe that He is and that He is a rewarder of them that diligently seek Him.

For those who are serious about growing in the knowledge of God and how to walk in the Spirit I would suggest reading and studying the book of Proverbs. It is truly helpful in learning how to walk in a serious relationship with God. Ask God to teach you as you spend time with Him and in His word. He will help you learn and grow in Him.

PROVERBS 3:5-13

Trust in the Lord with all thine heart and lean not unto thine own understanding.

In all thy ways acknowledge Him and He shall direct thy paths.

Be not wise in thine own eyes: fear the Lord and depart from evil.

It shall be health to thy navel (body) and marrow to thy bones.

Honor the Lord with all thy substance and with the first fruits of all thine increase:

So shall thy barns be filled with plenty and thy presses shall burst out with new wine (wine is a sign of power).

My son, despise not the chastening of the Lord; neither be weary of His correction:

> For whom the Lord loveth He correcteth; even as a father the son in whom He delighteth.
>
> Happy/blessed is the man that findeth wisdom and the man that getteth understanding.

I have read through the book of Proverbs quite a few times and every time I learn new things that help me in my walk with Him. There are so many wonderful promises in God's word that we can claim every day in our walk with Him. If you are being corrected because of some behavior or words that you use or anger, be thankful because He corrects us because He loves us so much and wants to help us. So remember we are never alone, we do not walk alone or grow in the knowledge of God alone. He is right there with us every step of the way. God teaches us through the help and guidance of the Holy Spirit. God in Christ in us through the Holy Spirit.

### JOSHUA 1:9

> Have not I commanded thee? Be strong and of a good courage, be not afraid, neither be thou dismayed for the Lord thy God is with thee whithersoever thou goest.

God is always with us through the power of Jesus Christ through the Holy Spirit. Through the death and resurrection of Jesus Christ we have access to all Jesus died for us to have. God has given us all that Jesus Christ is and we are all able to enjoy all He wants us to have. Believing, faith-filled believing is what makes us who we are in Christ. The Holy Spirit dwells in our spirit as He teaches and helps us to walk with the Holy Father to do His will for His pleasures. As we pray and study, we will see God working in us changing us and making us what He wants us to be. God blesses us as we grow in the knowledge of Him with faith filled believing.

EPHESIANS 1:17-19

That the God of our Lord Jesus Christ, the Father of glory, may give unto you the spirit of Wisdom and Revelation in the knowledge of Him:

The eyes of your understanding (heart) being enlightened; that ye may know what is the hope of His calling and what the Riches of the glory of His inheritance in the saints (believers).

And what is the exceeding greatness of His power to us-ward who Believe according to the working of His mighty power.

I pray God opens the heart of your understanding in wisdom and revelation in the true knowledge of Him. God is so good and He wants us to let His goodness work in us and then bless others.

Trust God and do good unto others is our purpose and His will for us in our daily walk.

GALATIANS 6:9

And let us not be weary in well- doing: for in due season we shall reap if we faint not.

If we trust God and do good unto others, we will produce fruit and reap reward. When the word of God talks about producing fruit it is talking about bringing others into fellowship with God by our example. This is our ultimate purpose in Him. God grants the increase, but we are His workman who needeth not to be ashamed. See Acts 2:47, 5:14, 6:7, 11:21, 16:5, 1 Corinthians 3:5-7.

Faith-filled believing is our key to open the most precious door available to us. Believing, Believing in the word of God and His son Jesus Christ and the Holy Spirit.

> LUKE 4:4
>
> And Jesus answered him, saying, It is written, that man shall not live by bread alone, but by every word of God.
>
> Luke 8:50
>
> But when Jesus heard it, He answered him saying, Fear Not; *believe only* and she shall be made whole.

Jesus did not only say that to them He is saying it to us, only believe! He wants us to open that most precious door with believing and enjoy all He has made available to all believers. Ask God to help you see what is available to us through Jesus Christ and search the scriptures daily.

> MATT 21:22
>
> (Jesus said) And all things, whatsoever ye shall ask in prayer, Believe, ye shall receive.

I wrote this in 1991 and want to share it with you. My son, my first child, was born when I was six months pregnant. He was born 2 lbs. 9 oz's. and dropped down to 1 lb. 9 oz's. He was in intensive care for about ten weeks and had two complete blood transfusions. By the time he was thirteen he had about 14 surgeries some being major. God is amazing!

## AUGUST 9, 1991

This summer has turned around quite differently.
My son's surgery has come along very significantly.
His recovery was quick and his release was swift.
His progress has been remarkable, no myth.

God has been with us through and through.
Two weeks they said his release would be due.
But four and a half days he was home and doing great.
God has made this such an incredibly short wait.
Not two weeks, but four and a half days, quite a result.
Our faith and belief in God's power, in bulk.
To share, God in Christ in us.
In God put all your love and trust.
For with Him the accomplishments are super.
He can help us to be such spiritual troopers.
God has blessed us so much.
With His wonderful love and amazing touch.
How can anyone know His ways?
When He has generously blessed our days.

My son was eleven years old when he had this major surgery. One of the problems he had was his growth center in his hip and his knee did not grow right due to an infection. He had so many other issues basically that one got missed. He ended up with one leg shorter than the other. Then there were surgeries trying to correct and lengthen his shorter leg. My son is now 40 years old and going great. He is married with three beautiful girls, my granddaughters.

Believing and trusting God and doing good unto others will increase your faith and your blessings. God has helped me through some challenging situations helping me to stay stable in His confidence in good times and bad. I am confident in Him and He is with me and I am never alone.

JOSHUA 1:9

> Have I not commanded thee, be strong and of a good courage, be not afraid, for the Lord thy God is with thee whithersoever thou goest.

Believing with faith-filled believing will never fail you. If God be for us who can be against us (Romans 8:31).

Psalms 71:15

My mouth shall shew forth Thy righteousness and thy salvation all the day long: for I know not the numbers thereof.

Again, faith-filled believing is what opens the door to God in Christ in us in the Holy Spirit. Letting God lead you by the leading and prompting of the Holy Spirit is an amazing walk with God.

LUKE 17:21

Neither shall they say, lo here! Or lo there! For behold the kingdom of God is **within you.**

Isaiah 26:3

Thou will keep him in perfect peace, whose mind is stayed on Thee: because he trusteth in Him.

God can work in us to slowly change us step by step if we ask Him to. God wants close fellowship with us and wants us to enjoy our lives in good times and bad with Him on our side.

HEBREWS 10:23

Let us hold fast the profession of our faith without wavering: for He is faithful that promised.

As long as we do our part God will faithfully do His part. God is looking for people, believers who do love Him and trust Him completely. He is always taking care of us in everything.

Isaiah 49:10

They shall not hunger or thirst; neither shall the heat nor sun smite them: for He that hath mercy on them shall lead them, even by the springs of water shall He guide them.

As we learn and grow and develop our walk with God we become more aware as the Holy Spirit guides us. The only way we can learn and grow in our walk with God is to study His word, His son Jesus Christ and the Holy Spirit. Without an understanding and knowledge of God's word on these topics we will never develop this most important relationship in our lives. Walking with God in Christ in the Holy Spirit is a work in progress that is not always easy, but it is definitely worth it. Walking with God in Christ being led by the Holy Spirit in God's presence and in His will to love others is amazing! Loving others and caring and helping others is why we are here. We are here to represent God in Jesus. While Jesus was here He did the Fathers will, which is what we are supposed to do. That means loving others and helping them. There are so many people who need to see by our example God in Christ in the Holy Spirit. We are God's representatives through Jesus Christ. We are here to help bring people into a real relationship/fellowship with God.

JOHN 17:4-8

I have glorified You on the earth. I have finished the work which You have given Me to do.

And now O Father, glorify thou now Me with Thine own self With the glory which I had with Thee before the world was.

I have manifested Thy name unto the men which Thou gavest Me out of the world: Thine they were and Thou gavest them Me and they have kept Thy word.

> Now they have known that all things whatsoever Thou hast given Me are of Thee.
>
> For I have given unto them the words which Thou gavest Me; and they have received them and have known surely that I came out from Thee and they have Believed that Thou didst send Me.

The key to un-lock all that Jesus died for us to have is Believing. If we know and have an understanding of God's word, then we can walk with Him in joy and peace doing His will for our lives.

Our thoughts are very important and we have to intentionally keep God in our thoughts and heart in everything we do. Each day Keep God first in your thoughts and prayers as you grow in Him.

> ISAIAH 26:3
>
> Thou (God) will keep him in perfect peace, whose mind is stayed on Thee: because he trusteth in Thee.

God is there for us because He has given us all that Jesus Christ is. We pray to God in the name of Jesus and follow the leadings of the Holy Spirit. If He (Holy Spirit) puts someone or some situation on your heart and you do not know why, pray for them or that situation and follow the leading of the Holy Spirit. Why pray? Because following the leading in any situation and praying and following the Holy Spirit is only going to benefit you and that particular person or situation.

> MATTHEW 21:22
>
> And whatever things you ask in prayer, believing, you will receive.

ROMANS 15:13 - 16

Now the God of hope fill you with all joy and peace in believing, that ye may abound in hope, through the power of the Holy Spirit.

That I should be the minister of Jesus Christ to the Gentiles, ministering the gospel of God, that the offering up of the Gentiles might be acceptable, being sanctified by the Holy Spirit.

1 CORINTHIANS 2:9-10

But as it is written, Eye hath not seen, nor ear heard, neither have entered into the heart of man, the things which God hath prepared for them that love Him.

But God hath revealed them unto us by His Spirit: for the Spirit searchest all things, yea, the Deep things of God.

God knows us and knows our heart for Him. God searches the heart of man and wants to help us in all areas of our lives. He wants us to walk in love, to help others by being an example to them. Look for someone to be a blessing too!

ISAIAH 30:18

And therefore will the Lord wait, that He may be gracious unto you, and therefore will He be exalted, that He may have mercy upon you: for the Lord is a God of judgment: blessed are all they that wait for Him.

God wants to be good to us. He is directing our steps through the leading of the Holy Spirit. As we learn God's ways and walk in them, we are growing and developing in our walk with God. God in Christ in us through the Holy Spirit. Believing in God's word, faith-filled believing is powerful because then we can be led by the Holy Spirit with total confidence in the Rest of God.

HEBREWS 4:3

For we who have believed do enter into Rest, as He said,

When we learn and grow in the wisdom and knowledge of God's word, we will experience the peace that Jesus Christ left us. God's will for us is to Believe, learn, grow and develop in spiritual maturity. Then God works in our spirit through the Holy Spirit who is our helper, our advocate and our stand-by. We grow from faith to faith and glory to glory in the love of Jesus Christ. God has given us many, many promises and blessings through Jesus Christ our Lord. The more we fellowship with God and pray and talk to Him throughout our daily walk we develop our personal relationship with Him. God in Christ in us through the Holy Spirit!

MARK 9:23

Jesus said unto him, If thou canst believe, all things are possible to him that believeth.

JOHN 5:24

Verily, verily, I say unto you, He that heareth My word and believeth on Him that sent Me, hath everlasting life and shall not come into condemnation: but is passed from death unto life.

Believing is our key to open the doors of heaven and He will pour out for you, such blessings that there will not be room enough to receive it. God loves us so much and wants to bless those that are in Christ. God is our wonderful, amazing Holy Father who wants a close personal relationship with those who Believe. My joy and strength come from believing in our Lord Jesus Christ.

> 2 Peter 1:5-7
>
> And beside this, giving all diligence, add to your faith virtue, and to virtue knowledge:
>
> And to knowledge, temperance (self-control); and to temperance patience; and to patience, godliness;
>
> And to godliness brotherly kindness; and to brotherly kindness Charity.
>
> ACTS 24:16
>
> …. I, myself always strive to have a conscience without offense toward God and men.

We as mature Christian believers should always strive to not offend God and others using the gift of self- control and please do not get offended easily. God wants us to mature little by little as we grow in Him with Faith-filled believing.

> MATTHEW 21:21
>
> So, Jesus answered and said to them, Assuredly, I say to you, if you have faith and do not doubt, you will not only do what was done to the fig tree, but also if you say to this mountain, Be removed and cast into the sea, it will be done.

Believing and trusting God is so powerful!

## ROMANS 8:29-31

For whom He did foreknow, He also did predestinate (us) to be conformed to the image of His Son, that He might be the firstborn among many brethren.

Moreover whom He did predestinate (us), them He also called ((us), and whom He called, them He also justified: and whom He Justified, them He also glorified.

What shall we then say to these things? If God be for us who can be against us?

1 Thessalonians 5:23-24

And the very God of Peace sanctify you wholly and I pray God your whole spirit and soul and body be preserved blameless unto the coming of our Lord Jesus Christ.

Faithful is He that calleth, Who also will do it.

God in Christ in us is our hope, our joy, our peace and our privilege because He first loved us. Living with Faith-filled believing in our Holy Father through our Lord Jesus Christ in every area of our lives trusting God and doing good unto others, is an amazing walk with Him.

# CHAPTER 2

## Trusting God

PSALMS 56: 3-4

What time I am afraid, I will trust in Thee.

In God I will praise His word, in God I have put my trust; I will not fear what flesh (man) can do unto me.

HEBRWS 13: 20-21

Now the God of Peace, that brought again from the dead our Lord Jesus, that great shepherd of the sheep, through the blood of the everlasting covenant,

Make you perfect in every good work to do His will, working in you that which is well pleasing in His sight, through Jesus Christ; to Whom be glory for ever and ever. Amen.

Through Jesus Christ we are complete in Him. We have everything we need to do God's work. Trust and believe in God, in Jesus Christ and in His word through the Holy Spirit. God is looking for people in all walks of life to be His laborers. His work for us is to love others as Jesus Christ did. Jesus is our example and we should study His word and how He handled various situations in the word. He prayed always and stopped to help people, love them, and heal them. Jesus talked to the Father all the time, as we should do throughout our day. If we keep God's word in our heart's we will listen to Him and do His work. Jesus tells us to keep His commandments if we love Him.

JOHN 14:15

If you love Me keep My commandments.

JOHN 14:21

He who has My commandments and keeps them, it is he who loves Me, and he who loves Me will be loved by My Father and I will love him and manifest Myself to him.

EPHESIANS 2:16-20

And that He might reconcile both (the old man and sin) unto God in one body (Jesus) by the cross, having slain the enmity, thereby;

And came and preached peace to you which were afar off and to them that were nigh.

For through Him (Jesus) we both (Jesus and us) have access by one Spirit unto the Father.

Now therefore ye are no more strangers and foreigners, but Fellow-Heirs with the saints and of the Household of God;

And are built upon the foundation of the apostles and prophets, Jesus Christ Himself being the chief corner stone.

EPHESIANS 3:17-20

That Christ may dwell in your Hearts by Faith (believing), that ye being rooted and grounded in love (God's love in Christ),

May be able to comprehend with all saints what is the breadth and length and depth and height.

And to know the love of Christ, which passeth knowledge, that ye might be filled with all the fulness of God.

Now unto Him (God) that is able to do exceeding abundantly above all that we ask or think according to the power (God in Christ in us in the Holy Spirit) that worketh in us.

We have power through God in Christ in us in the Holy Spirit in believing. Trusting God and believing His word has helped me in many different situations in my life. Being rooted and grounded in God's word is a must for mature believers. It gives you what you need to live day by day in peace and in His presence.

I talked about my son earlier and shared a poem I wrote when he had one of many surgeries. We all have to realize that we cannot lean unto our own understanding, but we can trust God with faith-filled Believing. Knowing in our hearts that He can do exceedingly abundantly above all we ask or think. Do not be wise in your own eyes. Pride is from the enemy and it will keep you from a wonderful walk with God. Stay strong in the Lord and the Power of His Might (not your might). Please do not fall into the trap of pride = defeat!

PROVERBS 16:18

Pride goeth before destruction and a haughty spirit before a fall.

WHICH WAY DO I GO?    6/28/1992

I believe that God will let me know.
When it's time, me, He will show.
The path that is right for little old me.
For He knows much better than us you see.
The best road or choice for our life.
Leaving behind all the worry and strife.
Having Faith and Trust in our Lord above.
As the Holy Spirit works within, with love.
As long as I stick with God and His word.
Our lives can't miss, haven't you heard.
He Blesses us all the time night and day.
What a wonderful life, it is the only way.
Thank you, Lord with all my Heart.

God has our back as we lean on and believe and trust that our lives and times are in His hands. He enables us through the Holy Spirit to handle all the different situations we encounter in our life. One day at a time is the only way we should live. We need to leave the past in the past and keep moving forward. If you are in Christ Jesus, then you know He has forgiven you of your past sins.

ISAIAH 42:9

Behold, the former things are come to pass and new things do I declare, before they spring forth I tell you of them.

With Faith-filled believing we keep moving forward in Christ Jesus. Trusting and believing that God has a unique plan for our lives. The more we know the word the more we know God and the heart of God for our lives. God wants us to walk in His love and to let that love flow through us to others. Remember, God wants us to love others because we love and trust Him. Loving others is part of who God is and what He wants us to do, as He stated in

1 PETER 1:22

Seeing ye have purified your souls in obeying the truth through the Spirit unto unfeigned (genuine) love of the brethren, see that ye love one another with a pure heart fervently.

That is our purpose in life, to love and help others as He loves and helps us. There are a lot of hurting people in the world who need our help. We are God's examples and representatives on this earth. He has us all strategically placed on the earth, so we can do the work He has called us to do.

PSALMS 18:30 (NLT)

God's way is perfect. All the Lord's promises prove true. He is shield for all who look to Him for protection.

God is our refuge and a stronghold in our lives. He keeps us anchored in His love. He is our high tower as it says in Psalms. God watches over us day and night as we walk with Him. He is our strength, our hope, and our everlasting Savior. For us to walk as He would have us walk, we need to know God's word and what it says about us. What God's word says about us and us in Christ are areas in God's word we should learn and study. That is how we know how much God loves us and provides for us, each and everyday. As we get to know God's word, we see how much He loves us and takes care of us. No matter what the current situations in our lives, we can go to Him anytime, anywhere. He is always there for us. God is our Rock and our Stronghold.

> PSALMS 91:15-16 (KJV)
>
> He shall call upon Me and I will answer him: I (God) will be with him in trouble; I will deliver him and honour him.
>
> With long life will I sanctify him and show him My salvation.

When we are concerned about various situations in our lives the first place we should go, before we go anywhere else, go to God first. Share with Him your situation and follow the leading of the Holy Spirit. Follow what He leads you to do. You may not get your answer right away but wait on the Lord your God because He will not leave you stuck. He will be there to help and take care of you and your life.

> 2 Corinthians 4:17 (NLT)
>
> For our present troubles are small and won't last very long. Yet they produce for us a glory that mostly outweighs them and will last forever!

God is our help when the storms of life come and they will come.

But if we trust Him with faith-filled believing the troubles that come will depart as God leads us by the Holy Spirit. God in us in Christ through the Holy Spirit! As we grow in God's word and His love it will get easier. The more you know God's word the more you develop a better understanding of how much God loves us and is always there to deliver us in all and any situation. God wants us to develop in Godly wisdom and understanding so we can walk in peace knowing He is always there through our spirit and in our heart. God is our sufficiency in all areas in our life. (2 Corinthians 3:4-6, 2 Corinthians 1:9)

God is our sufficiency in all areas of our lives because we are His children. Trusting God is the believer's response because He first loved us. (1 John 4:9) Our walk with God continues to grow and develop as we study God's word. We are His chosen people and He will guide us as we step out and believe His word.

> 2 SAMUEL 22:31-33
>
> As for God, His way is perfect: the word of the Lord is tried: He is a buckler to all them that Trust in Him.
>
> For who is God, save the Lord? And who is a rock, save our God?
>
> God is my strength and Power: and He maketh my way perfect.

I have learned over the years that I can Trust God in the good times and especially in bad times because He carries me through all times. He is my Rock, my shield, my fortress and keeps my heart anchored in His love and truth. God is my GPS in life. He directs me and guides my steps through all life throws at me and He keeps me stable. I told you earlier that my son had many surgeries due to being born premature. Through them all we believed and prayed and trusted God to bring him through wonderfully and He did! I wrote this poem in 1991 to thank all the faithful believers who prayed with us and for us.

### 6/26/1991

To all those who prayed for my son, God bless you!
I want to thank you all very much.
God has blessed my son and I with His loving touch.
Surgery went really great and is now over.
We all know it wasn't luck as in a four-leaf clover.
It is only the day after surgery and already,
My son has been up and walked the parallel bars, pretty steady.

Our prayers, love and trust in the Father.
Made today wonderful to be a part of.
My sons feeling great and healing rather quickly.
God sure makes my heart so tickly.
It is so wonderful how He works when we believe.
And that in itself, is such a relief.
All the surgeries he has ever had and this one.
I have claimed blessings through Jesus Christ, God's only begotten Son.
We haven't worried, but totally believed it would be fine.
God's been with us through every moment of this time.
Continually healing my son quickly, keeping wrinkles off my face.
Because worrying I will not, not even a trace.
Our Lord is always there.
Our Lord He really cares.

I have been walking with God for many years and have learnt that there is power in Believing. Yes, Believing in our Lord Jesus Christ and being led by the Holy Spirit. Trusting God and believing equals the power we are given through the resurrection of Jesus Christ. Jesus died so we could be saved and have all that He died for us to have. He also died so we could walk with Him in Peace and Joy. Peace equals power. Jesus does not want us to walk in worry or anger or un-forgiveness or frustration no matter what our situation is. If we can walk and keep our peace in good times and bad, we will experience the joy of the Lord in our hearts. Yes, if we are having problems, which we all do, then we should be praying, talking to God in Jesus name and praise Him and Thank Him for taking care of us, and He will! Let the Holy Spirit lead you and guide you each step of the way and He will help you through. That enables us to keep our peace and joy as a mature faith-filled believers in Christ Jesus. God in Christ in us. If you look at Jesus and how He walked with the Father, He always kept His peace even unto death and prayed for those who hurt Him.

JOHN 16:33

These things I have spoken unto you, that in Me ye might have peace. In the world ye shall have tribulation; but be of good cheer; I have over- come the world.

JOHN 14:27

Peace, I leave with you, My peace I give unto you; not as the world giveth, give I unto you. Let not your heart be troubled, neither let it be afraid.

Jesus left us His peace and tells us we will have tribulations, but we are to continue walking in the peace of Jesus Christ. Whatever you do, if you do not have peace about it, it is the Holy Spirit nudging you not to do it. If you follow the leading of the Holy Spirit you will know in your heart of hearts whether or not you have peace about something. God wants us to grow spiritually, so we can follow the leading of the Holy Spirit and walk in the love of Christ.

1 SAMUEL 25:6

And thus shall ye say to him that liveth, Peace both to thee and peace to thine house and peace unto all that thou has.

There are so many wonderful benefits that come with walking with God and growing in His word and the knowledge of Him. God's word tells us a lot about walking in Peace and trusting God and all His wonderful benefits walking in Him. God is our stronghold and fortress and our Peace.

EPHESIANS 1:3

Blessed be the God and Father of our Lord Jesus Christ, who has blessed us with All spiritual blessings in the Heavenly places in Christ.

PSALMS 72:17

His name shall endure forever, His name shall continue, as long as the sun: and men shall be blessed in Him: all nations shall call Him blessed.

We Are heirs of God through Jesus Christ. God wants us to be blessed and to know who we are in Christ. We are sons and daughters of the most high God through our Lord Jesus Christ. We also have responsibilities as sons and daughters with Christ. We are mature believers and should know who we are in Christ.

ROMANS 8:17

And if children, then heirs, heirs of God and joint heirs with Christ; if so be that we suffer (troubles/difficult times) with Him, that we may also be glorified together.

If we love God in good times and bad times, as His heirs with Christ, we will walk in joy and peace and be led by the Holy Spirit. We will enjoy our day to day walk with God. We will walk in the will of God and be His children and He will be our Father.

PSALMS 103:1-5

Bless the Lord, O my soul and all that is within me, bless His Holy name. Bless the Lord O my soul and forget not <u>All His benefits</u>. Who forgiveth all thine iniquities; who healeth all thy diseases. Who redeemeth thy life from destruction, who crowneth thee with loving kindness and tender mercies; who satisfieth thy mouth with good, thy youth is renewed like the eagles.

The love of God is so precious and He wants us to know He will never leave us nor forsake His children. Walk in the will of God through Jesus Christ and we will never be disappointed. God wants nothing, but the best for us, His children in our Lord Jesus Christ. God wants us to walk in His rest in everything we do. He wants us to walk and talk with Him through our day in His Rest.

HEBREWS 4:3

For we which have believed Do enter into Rest, as He said, as I have sworn in My wrath, if they shall enter into My Rest, although the works were finished from the foundation of the world.

God's rest is so amazing. Walking with God and trusting Him completely is how we can walk in His rest. If you do not put your trust in God, you may never accomplish walking in His rest. God knows our hearts and He knows if we Believe and trust in Him. Walking with God in His rest no matter what our circumstances are is immensely pleasing to God.

I would like to touch upon the subject of the enemy, the devil. As mature believers we should be aware that we have an enemy who wants to steal our peace and joy in Christ.

JOHN 10:10

The thief cometh not, but for to steal, and to kill, and to destroy: I am come that they might have life, and that they might have it more abundantly.

Jesus came so we could enjoy our lives with Him. The devil wants to steal, kill, and destroy our relationship with Him. That is why we need to stand firmly rooted and grounded in the word of God. Then when we are attacked, we can access the word and we are able to stay in the rest of God. We do that by believing and trusting God. Then we can say, it is written. That is how Jesus handled the devil, with the word of God. When we are having troubles in life, we know it comes from the enemy. That is why the word says,

We wrestle not against flesh and blood, but against principalities and power, against the rulers of the darkness of this world. Against spiritual wickedness in high places.

Wherefore take unto you the whole armor of God that ye may be able to withstand in the evil day, and having done all, to stand.

We have the armor of God. It is not physical armor, but spiritual armor because we wrestle not against flesh and blood. God has equipped us to fight in the spiritual realm. We have the belt of truth, the breastplate of righteousness, the shoes of peace, the shield of faith, and the sword of the Spirit, which is the word of God. God has given us through Jesus Christ all we need to defeat the attacks of the devil. So, therefore stand and be strong in the Lord and in the power of His might. That is why we need to be rooted and grounded in God's word and His love. His love for us is so powerful. Jesus gave us power and authority over the devil.

LUKE 9:1

Then He called His disciples together and gave them power and authority over all devils and to cure diseases.

We are Jesus' disciples, and we too have power and authority over the enemy through Jesus Christ. We should be all that Jesus died for us to be. To walk in the power and authority we have in Christ Jesus to defeat the works of the enemy. Put on the whole armor of God and stand, God will fight our battles for us, but we have to stand and stand firm in believing and trusting Him and stay in His rest. We need to thank and praise God daily for Jesus Christ and for all that He has made available to us in this day and time. It all comes down to believing and trusting God, Jesus Christ and God's word. Believing and trusting God is powerful. We have power and authority in Christ Jesus our Lord. Love never fails.

> 2 CORINTHIANS 13:11
>
> Finally, brethren, Farewell (Paul is speaking). Become complete. Be of good comfort, be of one mind, live in peace and the God of love and peace will be with you.
>
> EPHESIANS 2:14
>
> For He Himself is our peace who has made both and has broken down the middle wall of partition between us.

Believe and Trust in God and walk in the ways of Jesus Christ and He shall direct your path. He is our Rock and our stronghold in the day of trouble. Stand and keep your peace doing all that crisis demands, Stand.

> EPHESIANS 4:3 (AMP)
>
> Endeavoring to keep the unity of the Spirit in the bond of peace.

Believe and trust God and His word and walk with Him daily. He will keep you in peace and love as you walk with Him daily.

# CHAPTER 3

## Forgiveness

There are many things that hinder the workings of the Holy Spirit. Satan uses each one of them to trip us up. Such things as, doubt, worry, fear, criticizing others and judging them, talking about people behind their back and selfishness and self-centeredness. The biggest one he uses is un-forgiveness. Un-forgiveness prevents the working of the Holy Spirit from working in your spirit. I never want to stop the flow of the Holy Spirit in my life.

The leading of the Holy Spirit in our spirit is so wonderful and amazing. It helps us in our walk in the Rest of God in everything we do.

> 1 CORINTHIANS 2:9-12
>
> But as it is written, Eye hath not seen nor ear heard, neither have entered into the heart of man, the things which God hath prepared for them that love Him.
>
> For what man knoweth the things of a man, save the spirit of man which is within him? Even so the things of God knoweth no man, but the Spirit of God.

> Now we have received, not the spirit of the world, but the Spirit which is of (from) God; that we might know the things that are Freely Given to us of God.

Keeping the Holy Spirit working through our spirit is what helps us to walk pleasing to God in peace. Those walking in un-forgiveness will stop the Holy Spirit working in them. Jesus forgives us daily for our sins and iniquities. We repent and ask and receive forgiveness and keep moving forward in God's work. We all sin and come short of the glory of God. But there is now, no condemnation to those who are in Christ Jesus. If Jesus wants us to love others (which He does) then we should be able to forgive one another. Un-forgiveness is like poison in our lives. It affects our walk with God and obviously that is not God's will for you or me to have things hindering our walk with Him.

### COLOSSIANS 3:13

> Forbearing one another and forgiving one another, if any man have a quarrel against any: even as Christ forgave you, so also do ye.

God's word tells us to forgive because it benefits us. It brings us back to walking with Him in Peace. Forgiving others is one of the best things you can do to have a blessed life and keep the Holy Spirit flowing in your spirit.

### MARK 11:25

> And when ye stand praying, forgive, if ye have aught against any: that your Father also which is in heaven may forgive you your trespasses.

I am like everyone else and mess up from time to time. When I do I want God to forgive me. But, if I have un-forgiveness against anyone and do not forgive them, then God is not going to forgive me. But if I pray and ask God to help me forgive others and repent I can receive His forgiveness and move forward.

LUKE 6:35-38

But love your enemies and do good and lend, hoping for nothing again and your Reward shall be great and ye shall be the children of the Highest: for He is kind unto the unthankful and the evil.

Be ye therefore merciful, as your Father also is merciful.

Judge not and ye shall not be judged: condemn not and ye shall not be condemned: forgive and ye shall be forgiven:

Give and it shall be given unto you: good measure, pressed down and shaken together and running over, shall men give into your bosom. For with the same measure that ye mete (measure) withal it shall be measured to you again.

God not only wants us to forgive those who have hurt us, but He wants us to pray for them and love them and bless them. Forgiving others and praying for them opens the windows of heaven so, God can bless us and our reward will be great. So, you see, forgiving and praying for others blesses us and loads us with benefits and blessings and rewards. Hanging on to un-forgiveness is bitterness to the soul and prevents us from being led by the Holy Spirit.

Un-forgiveness holds us back, just as doubt, worry, fear and criticizing others and judging others. They all interfere with our walk with God. But un-forgiveness is what the enemy uses to keep us from the will of God. Satan knows all the tricks to disrupt our true purpose, the will of God. To love others and help them and pray for them, even our enemies.

PROVERBS 1:5

A wise man will hear and will increase in learning; and a man of understanding shall attain unto wise counsels:

PROVERBS 2: 1-5

My son, if thou wilt receive my words and hide my commandments with thee;

So that thou incline thine ear unto wisdom and apply thine heart to understanding;

Yea, if thou criest after knowledge and liftest up thy voice for understanding;

If thou seekest her (the word) as silver and searchest for her (the word) as for hidden treasures;

Then shalt thou understand the fear (reverence) of the Lord and find the knowledge of God.

If we seek God, we will find Him and as we seek the truth of God's word, we will find it. As you grow in the knowledge of God's word you will see and understand there is no place for un-forgiveness in our lives. All it does is steal our peace and joy. If you are not walking in peace, then you realize you are not truly walking with God. God wants us to forgive others so we can walk in peace with Him and not waste our time and energy in un-forgiveness. Do not let Satan use his devices to steal your peace and joy.

PROVERBS 3:1-3

My son, forget not My law; but let thine heart keep My commandments;

> For length of days and long life and Peace shall they add unto thee.
>
> Let not mercy and truth forsake thee: bind them upon the tablet of thine heart:
>
> So shalt thou Find favor and good understanding in the sight of God and man.

Study to know God's word, read books on the word or subjects you want to grow in regarding the Bible, the word of God. I continue to learn and grow in God's word daily. I read the Bible or books written about the Bible because I want to keep growing in the knowledge of Him. I read different sections in the Word of God that I have read before and find new things all the time. As I walk with Him daily, He works in me and teaches me things. He works to me and through me helping me to change where I need to, so I can be a blessing to others.

We are God's representatives and if we walk in un-forgiveness we are not being godly examples and representatives.

God's word, tell us in Proverbs "her ways" meaning the Word of God, are peace.

> PROVERBS 3:17
>
> Her ways are of pleasantness and all her paths are Peace.

If you need help with un-forgiveness with someone, I pray you studied God's word in that area and tap into other resources on forgiving others because it is so important. God is our vindicator, not we of ourselves. If we do our part, God most certainly will do His. Trust God and do Good!

ISAIAH 54:17

No weapon that is formed against me shall prosper; and every tongue that shall rise against thee in judgment Thou (God) shall condemn. This is the heritage of the servants of the Lord and their righteousness is of Me, saith the Lord.

There are many other scriptures on forgive and forgiving others and that tell you who you are in Christ. They can help you in your walk with God and living in His will in Peace.

Psalms 32:5
Psalms 99:8
Genisis50:17
1 Kings 8:30 AMP
Psalms 25:18
Psalms 86:5
Psalms 103:3
Matthew 5:44-45
Luke 6:35-38
Jeremiah 31: 33-34

Those are a few scriptures regarding forgive and forgiveness, which you can look and search these daily to see if they are true.

There is one sin in the word of God that say's, it will not be forgiven. This is an important scripture to know and understand with wisdom and Peace.

MATTHEW 12: 31-32

Wherefore I say unto you (Pharisees), all manner of sin and blasphemy shall be forgiven unto men: but the blasphemy against the Holy Spirit shall not be forgiven unto men.

> And whosoever speaketh a word against the Son of man it shall be forgiven him: but whosoever speaketh against the Holy Spirit it shall not be forgiven him, neither in this world, neither in the world to come.

God not only said once that blasphemy against the Holy Spirit will not be forgiven, He repeats it. He states it twice. First, God tells us in Matthew 2: 31, that all sins shall be forgiven except blasphemy against the Holy Spirit, He then repeats it in VS. 32. When God repeats something in His word it is something we should pay attention to and understand. God wants us to know all His word, not just little tid-bits here and there. Never blasphemy against the Holy Spirit if you truly love God and His word. He is our life source, all energy and peace and joy in our daily life. God in Christ in us Through the Holy Spirit.

If you are walking around with unforgiveness you will be unable to claim and walk in the promises of God and His word.

> HEBREWS 12: 1-2
>
> Wherefore seeing we also are compassed about with so great a cloud of witnesses (all who did in Chapter 11, we are still surrounded with their examples of trusting God), let us lay aside every weight and the sin which doth so easily beset us, and let us run with patience the race that is set before us,
>
> Looking unto Jesus the author and finisher of our faith; who for the joy that was set before Him endured the cross, despising the shame and is set down at the right hand of the throne of God.

Jesus died for us, so we could walk and have close fellowship with Him through the Holy Spirit. Jesus suffered, I mean really suffered, so we can live, laugh, and enjoy life and our daily walk with Him. That is so amazing!

EPHESIANS 3 17-20

That Christ may dwell in your hearts by faith; that ye being rooted and grounded in love,

May be able to comprehend with all saints what is the breadth, and length and depth and height;

And to know the love of Christ, which passeth knowledge, that ye may be filled with all the fullness of God.

Now unto Him (God) that is able to do exceedingly abundantly above all that we ask or think, according to the Power that worketh in us.

God wants us to know and comprehend the knowledge of Christ and His resurrection. Now we have the power of Christ working through us through the Holy Spirit. We are filled with all the fulness of God. He can do exceedingly abundantly above all that we ask or think through the power that works in us. God in Christ in us through the Holy Spirit.

If we do our part God will most certainly do His. The promises of God are for you and me and we need to walk in them and show the world who we are in Christ. We should be living a life that makes people say, I want what they have! Peace, joy, kindness, patience, trust, and total confidence in our heart. God is always working in us and for us in all things.

2 Corinthians 2:20

For all the promises of God in Him, yea, and in Him Amen, unto the glory of God by us.

God's promises are for all of us in Christ Jesus. God wants us to live in His word and in all His promises as we learn and grow in the knowledge of Him. It is so important to read and study God's word. If you have difficulty understanding God's word, there are plenty of resources out there to help you. Pray and ask God to help you and teach you as you walk with Him. God will help you as you pursue, to know Him. God knows your heart and He knows if you are diligently seeking Him.

God will help you and teach you as you diligently seek Him. Let the working of the Holy Spirit fill you and walk with you in everything.

>PSALMS 9:10

>And they that know Thy name will put their trust in Thee: for Thou, Lord, hast not forsaken thee.

As we walk with God and learn to trust Him and His word, we continually grow in the knowledge of Christ through seeking Him through the Holy Spirit. God wants us to go to Him first with everything. He hears and listens to us when we talk to Him and when we pray in Jesus name. No Man knoweth the Father except by Jesus Christ. Walk with God and He will walk with you in your daily journey in getting to know Him and the power of His might.

>COLOSSIANS 2:10

>And ye are complete in Him, which is the head of all principalities and power.

If you have a true heart for God, then keep moving forward and showing people by your example what a true faith-filled Christian is. Believing, behaving, and representing God in a crazy mixed up world.

>1 THESSALONIANS 1:9

>For they themselves show of us what manner of entering in we had unto you and how ye turned to God from idols to serve the living and true God.

Anything can be an idol if we put it before God. God wants to be our first thought in the morning and throughout our day. Your car, money, gaming systems and anything that comes before God is an Idol.

1 JOHN 3:18-21 (AMP)

> Little Children, it is the last time: and as ye have heard that antichrist shall come, even now are there many antichrists; whereby we know that it is the last time.
>
> They went out from us, but they are not of us; for if they had been of us, they would no doubt have continued with us; but they went out, that they might be made manifest that they were not all of us.
>
> But ye have an unction from the Holy One, and Ye know all things.
>
> I have not written unto you because ye know not the truth, but because ye know it and that no lie is of the truth.

We are to let our actions and behavior and attitudes speak louder than our words alone. We are in Christ Jesus and God is waiting for us to step up to the plate with all confidence and trust in Him. Thus, we can help others struggling to know Christ and help those who are hurting. One person at a time, then another, then another and another. Loving God, helping people and doing good to other people is who we are in Christ. We walk in the will of God through Jesus through the Holy Spirit. We are to love other people as we are instructed to do in God's word. We should be believing the best in and of people. Everyone has their own problems, even if you do not see them. Sometimes those problems disturb our peace, and we behave badly. We need to always believe the best with patience and understanding. The word of God says, love covers a multitude of sins.

1 PETER 4:8

And above all things have fervent charity (love) among yourselves: For charity shall cover the multitude of sins.

If someone offends you or hurts you, try not to get offended. The word tells us to cover their sin, forgive and ask God to help you and move on. Try believing the best and let love cover the sin or offence. We should not be telling the world about the situation and gossiping and complaining about it. If you do that then how can you move forward? That is not God's will for us or for others. Go to God pray/talk to Him and ask Him to help you and take that right out of you. Then you can continue walking with God in peace and joy and fellowship. I know, for myself, I do not want anything to Steal my peace and joy. That is exactly what Satan is trying to do. DO NOT LET HIM!

DEUTERONOMY 20:4

For the Lord God is He that goeth with you to fight for you against your enemies, to save you!

Let God fight your battles for you. Go to Him first talk to Him about your situation and let Him help you. Go to God with praise and thanksgiving for always being there for you.

ROMANS 15:13

Now the God of hope fill you with all joy and peace in believing, that ye may abound in Hope, through the Power of the Holy Spirit.

I pray you work on not letting anyone or anything steal your joy and peace. As you walk in the spirit God will walk with you through all your ups and downs.

MARK 11:25

And when ye stand praying, forgive, if ye have aught against any: that your Father also which is in heaven may forgive you your trespasses.

We forgive others so we can be blessed. God has given us what we need to defeat the devil and walk in His love.

God tells us in the KJV not to be ignorant of the devils devices and that will help us to be more than conquers.

ROMANS 1:3 (AMP)

Now I would not have you ignorant, brethren, that often- times I purposed to come unto you, (but was hindered hitherto – distracted by the enemy) that I might have some fruit among other Gentiles.

When Paul says have some fruit among the Gentiles, he is talking about added people into the church of God, but he was hindered by the devil. The devil does not want us doing the works of God and tries to hinder us every chance he has. That is why we are told not to be ignorant.

ROMANS 11:25

For I would not, brethren, that ye should be ignorant of this mystery, lest ye should be wise in your own conceits; that blindness (pride blinded them) in part has happened to Israel, until the fulness of the Gentiles be come in.

The mystery Paul is talking about is the hardness of Israel's heart was made known. It is God in Christ in us through the Holy Spirit. The devil wants to steal our relationship with God.

## 1 CORINTHIANS 10:1

MOREOVER, brethren, I would not that ye should be ignorant, how that all our fathers were under the cloud, and all passed through the sea.

The devil hindered all Israel in all their journeys trying and keeping them from God. They were led astray by the enemy so many times and it displeased God tremendously.

## 1 CORINTHIANS 12:1

Now concerning spiritual matters, brethren, I would not have you ignorant.

Spiritual matters are all that God through His mercy and grace gave us to defeat the devil and help others.

## 2 CORINTHIANS 2:11

Lest Satan should get an advantage of us: for we are not ignorant of his devices.

We are not and should not be ignorant of the enemy's devices.

## 2 CORINTHIANS 1:8

For we would not, brethren, have you ignorant of our trouble which came to us, that we were pressed out of measure, above strength, insomuch that we despaired even of life.

The devil fights us all the way just as he did with Paul and the disciples. He attacks believers to keep them from the word of God.

## 1 THESSALONIANS 4:13

But I would not have you to be ignorant, brethren, concerning them which are asleep (dead), that ye sorrow not, even as others which have no hope.

Paul does not want us to be poor godly representatives when people pass away. We which are in Christ have the hope that He died for us to have. In all circumstances we are God's representatives. We that believe know we will see our loved ones again. That is the amazing hope that we have.

## ROMANS 10:3

For they, being ignorant of God's righteousness, and going about to establish their own righteousness, have not submitted themselves unto the righteousness of God.

We cannot lean unto our own understanding. The devil tries to pull people away from the righteousness we have from God in Christ. We are the righteousness of God in Christ through the Holy Spirit.

## EPHESIANS 4:18

Having their understanding darkened, being alienated from the life of God through the ignorance that is in them, because of the blindness of their heart.

The enemy got to them, and they hardened their hearts toward God. The devil is always working to trip believers up, which is why we need to put on the full armor of God so we can resist the fiery darts of the enemy. God's word tells us numerous times not to be ignorant. That is why God gave us His word. He wants us to know and understand what God has provided for us if we faint not.

# CHAPTER 4

## Trusting God And His Word

God has given us salvation through Jesus Christ. He has given us many gifts to help us in all situations through the Holy Spirit. Seek and keep on seeking, ask, and keep on asking and it will be given you. We have the gift of righteousness, the gift of grace, the gift of the Holy Spirit and the gift of eternal life, just to mention a few. We have remission of sins (Acts 2:38-38), we have the Fruit of the Spirit (Galatians 5:22-23) and many others we can be thankful for. The fruit of the Spirit is love, joy, peace, longsuffering (patience), gentleness, goodness, faith, meekness (humbleness), temperance (balance), against such there is no law (Galatians 5: 22-23).

God has blessed us with all spiritual blessings so we can walk with Him in peace and joy and hope.

> HEBREWS 6:19
>
> Which hope we have as an anchor of the soul, both sure and steadfast (fixed), and which entered into that within the veil;

Our soul is our mind, will, emotions and our feelings. We have an anchor for our soul life, the word of God, so our soul life and spiritual life can work together for the glory of God. As our soul life and our spiritual life comes into agreement in the knowledge of Him our life becomes more peaceful. We cannot let our emotions, or our feelings control us. We are in control, and we decide to either follow our feelings and emotions or we decide to follow God in Christ in us through the Holy Spirit. When things happen, we need to stay calm and think things through according to the word of God. Then you can stay in peace with faith-filled believing, trusting God to do what only He can do. If you are not walking in peace through the Holy Spirit, ask God to help you and teach you so you can get back to peace. If you are not in peace, ask God and He will help you to figure it out. If you have peace about a situation or decision the Holy Spirit is working in you. If you are not in peace, follow the leading of the Holy Spirit because He is trying to tell you something. God is not the author of confusion.

1 CORINTHIANS 14:33

> For God is not the author of confusion, but of peace, as in all churches of the saints (believers).

Peace has dynamic power and when we are walking in peace with the Holy Spirit it is Amazing and God's power through Jesus Christ through the Holy Spirit helps us in good times and bad.

Trust God and do good unto others, forgive, believe the best of others, and walk in peace and be blessed. I know I use this scripture a lot, but it is so important to know and walk in the word of God.

PHILIPPIANS 4:7

> And let the Peace of God, which passeth all understanding (human understanding not spiritual), shall keep your hearts and mind through Christ Jesus.

We are God's saints, believers whom He loves. God wants that love to flow to us and through us to others. God's love is loving and helping and taking care of other people just as God loves and takes care of us.

We are here at this particular time because God wants us to show His love in our everyday walk with Him. We are the lights in the world and God has placed us here strategically to produce good fruit, being His examples and representatives in this day and time.

We need to walk with God and in the Spirit of His might. Love One another, help God and walk in His will of loving others, lets help God and do the work He has set before us.

1 CORINTHIANS 13:13

> And now abideth in faith, hope, charity, these three; but the greatest of these is charity.

We have faith, hope and charity through Jesus Christ. Charity is love (AGAPE- love – God in Christ in me through the Holy Spirit in manifestation), so we can help those in need. Helping others is a very important part of our walk with God. If you have ever read the Bible God tells us numerous times to help the poor, needy and widows and fatherless. This tells me we are to help people in need.

1 CORINTHIANS 13:6-8a

> Rejoice not in iniquity, but rejoice in Truth, beareth all things, believeth all things, hopeth all things, endureth all things, Charity never faileth.

Forgive others and trust God and walk with God in Christ through the Holy Spirit. Walk in the spirit in the peace that passes carnal understanding. People around you will see you in constant peace and constant stability and will want what you have, God in Christ in you. Remember, Jesus has overcome the world (John 16:33) and has left us power and authority over the enemy. As you apply and walk in the fruit of the Holy Spirit (Galatians 5:22-33) you will walk in peace and enjoy your life. You will be stable through self-control and discipline, which is part of the fruit of the Spirit. You will walk in humbleness, kindness, forgiveness and contentment with confidence and trust in God. God's word is life changing as we grow and walk in it. God is there for us 24 hours a day seven days a week, so talk to Him and let Him be number one in your life. We should praise Him and thank Him daily for taking care of us. God has changed me over many years, and I am nothing like I used to be. I thank Him and Praise Him daily for all He has done in me. God is our stronghold, He is amazing, and He is Holy. We should walk in His Holiness through Jesus Christ through the Holy Spirit. He wants to help us in everything and bless us.

ISAIAH 30:18

And therefore, will the Lord wait, that He may be gracious (good) unto you, and therefore will He be exalted, that He may have mercy upon you, For the Lord is a God of judgment, blessed are they that wait for Him.

ROMANS 8:28

And we know that all things work together for good to them that love God, to them who are called according to His Purpose.

As we seek God and He is first in our lives, the Holy Spirit walks with us guiding us through our spirit. He is our helper and directs our steps through thick and thin. He Tells us many times to seek Him. We seek God because we love Him, who first loved us. We seek God because we want to know Him and desire a relationship with Him. We seek God to learn and grow in Him and to have fellowship with Him.

We seek Him and the Power of His might to change us and make us what He wants us to be. To know who we are in Christ because of His resurrection, so we can have all that He died for us to have. We praise God and with thankful hearts because He has blessed us with all spiritual blessings in the heavenly's. We seek Him daily so He can help us walk in the fruit of the Spirit and live a balanced, stable, confident walk with Him.

ACTS 17:27-28

That they should seek the Lord, if haply they might feel after Him, and find Him, though He be not far from every one of us;

For in Him we live and move and have our being; as certain also of your poets have said, for we are also His offspring.

It takes faith-filled believing to get to know God and see that He is always there for us. God in Christ in us in the Holy Spirit. We can Trust God in every area of our lives. He has plans for you to enjoy your life if you walk with Him with faith-filled believing.

HEBREWS 11:6

But without faith it is impossible to please Him; for he that cometh to God must believe that He is, and that He is a rewarder of them that diligently Seek Him.

As we spend time in God's word and walk and seek Him diligently, He will be gracious unto us. God knows our heart.

MATTHEW 7:7-8

Ask and it shall be given you, seek and ye shall find, knock and it shall be opened unto you.

For everyone that asketh receiveth; and he that seeketh findeth; and to him that knocketh it shall be opened.

God is just waiting and looking and longing for someone to bless. He wants us to walk with Him and He will strengthen us in our weaknesses. He is our peace and joy. God in Christ in us, that is what our walk should look like.

> JEREMIAH 29: 12-13
>
> Then shall ye call upon Me and ye shall go and pray unto Me and I will hearken unto you.
>
> And ye shall seek Me and find Me, when ye shall search for Me with all your heart.

God tells us to seek Him and search for Him with all our heart. God knows our heart and those that diligently seek Him because we trust Him and walk with Him daily with faith-filled believing in His word.

There have been many times when I have had to get control of my feelings and emotions. I have to use self-control and discipline and get back into peace not letting my feelings/emotions control me. I get back into fellowship with God and trust Him to work it out for my good. Then I can be in peace and do good unto others and pass it forward. I had to seek God and His peace and let it flow through me. Then and only then could I move forward in His love.

> PSALMS 22:26
>
> The meek (humble) shall eat and be satisfied: they shall praise the Lord that seek Him: your heart shall live forever.
>
> PSALMS 26:3
>
> For Thy loving kindness is before mine eyes and I have walked in thy truth (word),

I praise the Lord daily for His love, for taking care of me, and helping me to behave as a faith-filled believer. And when I mess up, as we all do, I repent, receive His forgiveness through Jesus Christ and move on walking with God as He helps me and corrects me. When God corrects us, He is letting us know He cares about us and everything we do. If He takes time to stop and correct us, we know He is always thinking about us all the time.

> PSALMS 40:5-6
>
> Many, O Lord my God are Thy wonderful works which thou hast done and Thy thoughts which are to us-ward: they cannot be reckoned up (counted) in order unto Thee: if I would declare and speak of them, they are more than can be numbered.
>
> Sacrifice and offering Thou didst not desire; my ears hast Thou opened: burnt offerings and sin offerings hast Thou not required.

In the Old Testament people had to make offerings and sacrifices for sins and trespasses. They had to offer burnt offerings and others. They did not have Jesus Christ as we do today. They worked hard and had to do all those sacrifices and offerings to God for a variety of different reasons. Jesus Christ was always God's plan to save us from that.

God thinks about us all the time. Can you say the same about Him? Do you think about God throughout your day? Do you walk in His presence in all you do? Do you seek God throughout your day? Do you pray and talk to God in whatever you are doing? God thinks about us in good times and bad. His thoughts to us-ward are uncountable.

> PSALMS 56:8-11
>
> Thou tellest my wanderings: put thou my tears into thy bottle: are thy not in Thy book? When I cry unto thee,

then shall mine enemies turn back: this I know; for God is for me. In God will I praise His word: In the Lord will I praise His word. In God have I put my trust: I will not be afraid what can man do unto me.

God never leaves us alone. He is with us, He is there to help us and to walk and talk with us. A mature faith-filled Christian walk is a lifestyle. We learn and grow and develop all that Christ died for us to have, then we walk in a faith-filled believing walk with God. A believer's walk is a day by day and step by step walk. And we learn to live as God would have us. It is a day by day walk learning to trust God and do good unto others. Trust God and do good walking in peace and confidence through Jesus Christ. Christ is our example of how we should act, talk, believe, pray and walk with God.

1JOHN 4:18

There is no fear in love, but perfect love casteth out fear: because fear hath torment. He that feareth is not made perfect in love.

If we love God, we have nothing to fear. If we walk in the love of God through Christ in the Holy Spirit, we will not be afraid. We are well aware, that If God be for us who can be against us. We walk in love and not in fear. If something comes up and you are fearful and un-peaceful bring it to God. Talk with God about it and let Him help you. Remember the word in your heart, speak it and believe and get back in peace.

LUKE 1:37

For with God nothing shall be impossible.

Pray and talk to God with confidence and faith-filled believing. God wants you to share your life with Him in all things. He is telling us if we walk with Him nothing is impossible. That is quite a promise we have from God. God is so amazing and full of grace and mercy to those that love Him and believe and trust in Him.

PSALMS 56:3

What time I am afraid, I will trust in Thee.

Trusting God is so powerful. Many people in God's word trusted in Him. There are many examples in the Old and New Testament. We can learn from all of them. Having time to read, study and know God's word and instruction and promises are so priceless. It helps us to learn and trust God and His power in us.

In 2 Chronicles, Jehoshaphat, is talking with God, He praises Him and lets Him know what he is dealing with from the enemy. Jehoshaphat is trusting God in times of troubles.

2 CHRONICLES 20: 12, 15

O our God, wilt thou not judge them? For we have no might against this great company that cometh against us; neither know we what to do: but our eyes are upon Thee.

And He said, Hearken ye, all Judah and ye inhabitants of Jerusalem, and thou king Jehoshaphat, Thus saith the Lord unto you, be not afraid nor dismayed by reason of this great multitude; for the battle is not yours, but God's.

2 CHRONICLES 20:17

Ye shall not need to fight in this battle: set yourselves, Stand ye still and see the salvation of the Lord with you, O Judah and Jerusalem: fear not nor be dismayed:

to-morrow go out against them: for the Lord will be with you.

2 CHRONICLES 20:22

And when they began to sing and to Praise, the Lord set ambushes against the children of Ammon, Moab, and mount Seir, which were come against Judah; and they were smitten.

If you read that particular story about that battle you will see God defeated their enemies. Jehoshaphat and his company were told to Stand, sing and Praise God and the enemy was self-slaughtered because they were so confused when they heard them praising and thanking God. They were defeated by their own armies.

God is so worthy to be praised, He is so amazing, trustworthy, and Holy.

# CHAPTER 5

## Walking with God

JEREMIAH 29:12

> Then ye shall call upon Me and ye shall go and pray unto Me, and I will hearken unto you.

As we walk with God and pray and talk with Him, He is telling us He will listen to us. How amazing is that, the God of the universe listens to us. Again, walking with God is a day to day journey, growing and learning and moving forward in God's abundant love and grace for us.

ISAIAH 41:10

> Fear thou not for I am with thee, be not dismayed, for I am Thy God, I will strengthen thee, yea, I will help uphold thee with the right hand of My righteousness.

God is always there waiting to help us through Jesus Christ in the Holy Spirit. He is telling us He will uphold us when we need it, and He will strengthen us and be with us. God through Jesus Christ in the Holy Spirit is and should be our sufficiency in everything.

MATTHEW 6:31-33

> Therefore, take no thought saying, what shall we eat? Or what shall we drink? Or wherewithal shall we be clothed? (His character).
>
> For after all these things do the Gentiles seek: for your heavenly Father knoweth that ye have need of all these things.
>
> But seek ye first the kingdom of God and His righteousness and all these things shall be added unto you.

God wants to bless us with much, but first we have to seek Him, His ways, His will and His character. God wants us to believe and trust His will and His ways in our lives. The only way to know God's will is to know His word, His promises to us, the gifts He has bestowed upon us and who we are in Jesus Christ through the Holy Spirit. God will show you amazing and wonderful things in your day to day walk with Him. Spend time in His word in a one on one relationship with God walking in fellowship with Him. Walking with God means just that! We talk with God throughout our day and thank Him and Praise His wonderful Holy name. We thank God for His grace and mercy and forgiveness. We praise Him for all He has made available to us through the death and resurrection of our Lord Jesus Christ.

1 CORINTHIANS 1:30

> But of Him are ye in Christ Jesus, who of God is made unto us wisdom and righteousness and sanctification and redemption (holiness set apart).

We have so much through Jesus Christ. Learning what the word says we have and learning to walk in Christ in the Holy Spirit. This is so important to learn and understand. Then walking in peace and joy gets easier and easier as we walk and talk with Him. God's word tells us how to behave and talk and please Him with our godly attitude. Walking in peace and balance and stability and joy and doing good unto others pleases God. It all starts with Believing and believing in the Word Of God. Godly wisdom through the Holy Spirit will help us in our daily walk with Him. Trusting and believing God is powerful in the spirit realm.

PROVERBS 10:23

It is as sport to a fool to do mischief; but a man of understanding hath wisdom.

We should use godly understanding and wisdom in all we do. The Word is our way to understanding and wisdom. Walking in godly wisdom as we go through our day will keep us in the power of peace and joy.

PROVERBS 1:2-5

To know wisdom and understanding; to perceive the words (the Word of God) of understanding;

to receive the instruction of wisdom, justice, and judgment and equity;

to give subtilty (wisdom) to the simple, to the young man knowledge and discretion.

A wise man will hear and will increase learning; and a man of understanding shall attain unto wise counsels.

As we increase in learning and walking with God through Jesus Christ through the Holy Spirit we grow in godly wisdom, knowledge and understanding. We walk with God in His will by knowing the word of God. We should know how to act, how to talk and behave as godly wise representatives of our Lord Jesus Christ in a confused and hurting world.

2 PETER 3:15

> And account (consider) that the long suffering of our Lord is salvation: even as our beloved brother Paul also according to the wisdom (revelation from God) given unto him hath **written unto you.**

God gave the word to Paul by revelation through the Holy Spirit to write down when he was in prison. Paul wrote God's word as the Spirit gave him revelation. God wants us to have His word so we can Know Him and walk with Him. God is always trying to teach us and guide our steps in His perfect will for us. If we are wise and in close daily fellowship with Him, you know this to be true.

JAMES 1:5

> If any of you lack wisdom, let him ask of God, that giveth to all men liberally and upbraideth not and it shall be given him.

God's will is for us to want His will and His ways. If we are searching, He is telling us to search for godly wisdom and understanding. Even though God knows our hearts we must ask Him for what we are lacking. That is part of walking in fellowship with our heavenly Father.

JAMES 3:13

> Who is a wise man and endued with knowledge among you? Let him show out of a good conversation his works with meekness of wisdom.

God is there with us as we study, research and work to understand with godly wisdom, His Word. God's love and His will for us is to love Him and walk with Him. It is an amazing walk of learning and growing in Him.

JAMES 3:17

But the wisdom that is from above is first pure, then peaceable, gentle and easy to be entreated, full of mercy and good fruits without partiality and without hypocrisy.

We walk with God in Christ in the Holy Spirit. God's wisdom is pure, peaceable, gentle, and easy and full of mercy and good fruits. God's word is full of riches and treasures and wonderful truths. If you believe with faith-filled believing you can have a wonderful walk with God. Let God work in your life changing you little by little from faith to faith and glory to glory. As the Holy Spirit works with your spirit you learn and grow, He opens the heart of your understanding. That is how we develop in His knowledge and wisdom for us and others.

ROMANS 5:5

And hope maketh not ashamed, because the love of God is shed abroad in our hearts by the Holy Spirit which is given unto us.

Jesus died and rose again and is now seated at the right hand of God. He died and was the last sacrifice that was ever needed. Jesus died so we could have remission of sins and be saved. Jesus sacrificed His life, so we no longer need sacrifices as they did in the Old Testament. When Jesus ascended into heaven and was seated at the right hand of God, He sent us the Holy Spirit to be there for us. God in Christ in us through the Holy Spirit is what Jesus Christ has accomplished for us.

JOHN 6:28-29

Then said they unto Him, what shall we do that we might work the works of God?

> Jesus answered and said unto them, This, is the work of God, that ye <u>believe</u> on Him (Jesus) whom He (God) hath sent.

Faith-filled believing in all that Jesus died for us to have, gives us the ability to do all things according to the will of God. It allows you to walk with God in fellowship through Jesus Christ in the Holy Spirit. We learn and grow as we walk in peace and joy and confidence in all God's word says to us. God has made us complete in Him. Thanking and praising God for all He has made available to us according to His word, we just have to receive it. Thanking God for all He has blessed us with. That is part of developing in spiritual maturity walking with God in His love believing and doing good unto others praising Him.

> PSALMS 100:4-5
>
> Enter into His gates with <u>thanksgiving</u> and into His courts with <u>praise</u>. Be <u>thankful</u> unto Him and bless His name.
>
> For the Lord is good His mercy is everlasting and His truth endureth to all generations.

Praising God for His goodness, His graciousness and His mercy for all He has taught us and opened up to us about Himself, His Son, and the Holy Spirit. Continue to Walk with Him being spiritually mature having a good knowledge and understanding of God's word. Then you can walk in peace in good times and bad. If you are struggling right now, slow down and talk to God and tell Him your situation and cast your care to Him and He will fight your battles. Thank Him and Praise Him and let Him bless you as you stay in Peace Trusting God.

I am going to remind you again that walking with God is a step by step and day by day walk. As He teaches us, we praise and thank His Holy name. He teaches us through His word about His ways and His character and His will. He teaches us how we should behave and talk and how to walk in His truth and love.

### PSALMS 34:3-4

O magnify the Lord with <u>me</u> and let <u>us</u> exalt His name <u>together</u>.

I sought the Lord and He heard me and delivered me from all my fears.

We are the church, people, and we should be walking in total confidence in God without doubt, worry or fear.

That confidence in God in Christ in us allows us to walk in peace instead of doubt, worry, and fear. If the enemy attacks you speak God's word to yourself or out loud and let Him know you are the righteousness of God through the blood of Jesus Christ. The Word is a weapon, the sword of the Spirit and when attacked we fight back with God's word. "It is written,"

### EPHESIANS 6:12

We wrestle not against flesh and blood but against principalities, against powers, against the rulers of the darkness of this world, against spiritual wickedness in high places.

People are used by the enemy, but we do not fight in the physical realm. We do not fight against flesh and blood. We fight in the spirit realm because that is where attacks come from. We put on our shoes of peace, the belt of truth, the helmet of salvation, the breastplate of righteousness (God in Christ in us) and the Sword of the Spirit (the Word of God). EPHESIANS 6: 14-17

When we know what the word of God says we can walk in the knowledge of Him. Without the word there is no other way to get to know God. The Bible, the word of God is still the best- selling book of all times. God wants us to know Him in our Heart of hearts. God wants us to Keep His word in our hearts so we can use it whenever we need it. When we know God's word we know how to walk and defeat the enemy in the spirit realm because we wrestle not against flesh and blood. That is loving God and walking in confidence in Him without fear or doubt or worry. That confidence in God in Christ in us allows us to walk in peace. Knowing God's word is the best way to fight in the spirit realm, with "it is written." Pray and talk to God and the Holy Spirit will help you. People and even your loved ones are vehicles for the enemy's attacks. Pray and always pray, seeking God and asking Him for His mighty hand to work in your situation. Trust me, if you are walking with Him in Christ the Holy Spirit will help you. He is always waiting and looking for someone to help and love.

ISAIAH 26:3

Thou will keep him in perfect peace, whose mind is stayed on You, Because he trusteth in You.

If God and His word is in your hearts and you daily walk with Him, He will keep you in peace. That is truly walking with God in all things. Because we trust in Him with Faith-filled believing in Christ through the Holy Spirit.

## CHAPTER 6

## Peace

God honestly wants us to be in peace. Jesus Christ did not die for us to be anxious, fearful, confused and miserable. He died so we could have and enjoy our life in abundance to the full and overflowing. (See John 10:10) That is only part of what we have in Christ. We have so much available to us in Christ including peace. The definition of peace is a calm, freedom from disturbance, tranquility, and an inner peace. Walking in peace, even though life gets crazy, may seem challenging, but that is where knowing God's word comes in.

> ROMANS 5:1
>
> Therefore, being justified by Faith we have peace with God through our Lord Jesus Christ.
>
> ROMANS 8:6
>
> For to be carnally minded is death, but to be spiritually minded (God in Christ in you) is life and peace.

We need to walk in the peace of Jesus Christ and the Rest of God. God's word tells us to walk in His rest. Mature Faith-filled believers should be enjoying their walk with God. God continually wants to help us and bless us as we walk in His will and in His word, then we can walk in His rest. The rest of God is not about rest from our daily activities, but in them. It is that profound peace that God gives to those who love and obey Him regardless of the circumstances. It is peace that involves the whole of your being, body, soul, mind, and spirit. It is not a rest from work, but a rest you have even when you are working. You know in your heart that you are walking and obeying God in all areas of your life. You believe God's word by Faith, and you enter into God's rest, and you cease from doubt, worry and fear. Trust God believe His word and walk in His rest.

HEBREWS 4:11

Let us labor therefore, to enter into Rest, lest any man fall after the same example of unbelief.

ROMANS 12:2

And be not conformed to this world: But be ye transformed by the renewing of your mind, that ye prove what is that good and acceptable and perfect will of God.

We trust God, obey Him, believe with all our heart's that He is able to do what He says He can do. Our walk is a daily walk with God. We renew our minds and hearts to His word. We lead everything into the captivity of Christ. Faith-filled believing in God in Christ in us through the Holy Spirit. You grow and mature in Him and in walking in the fruit of the spirit. Love, joy, peace, longsuffering (patience/endureth), gentleness, goodness, Faith, meekness, self-control (control under pressure), and temperance. (Galatians 5:22-23) We begin by studying God's word and growing in His love one step at a time. Unless you have a good knowledge and understanding of God's word walking in peace in all situations, is a worthy goal to achieve. A lot of the Epistles start with grace and peace be multiplied unto you from God our Father and our Lord Jesus Christ because Paul had achieved that goal. Paul wanted nothing more than to know Him and the power of His resurrection. He was well aware of the power available to us born again faith-filled believers. There is power when we utilize all the gifts and fruit of the Spirit. The Bible says, if we live in the spirit let us also walk in the Spirit (Galatians 5:25).

> ISAIAH 40:31
>
> But they that wait upon the Lord shall renew their strength, they shall mount up with wings as eagles, they shall run and not be weary and they shall not faint.
>
> ISAIAH 40:29
>
> He hath given power to the faint, and to them that have no might He increase strength.

God takes care of us in everything. He strengthens us when we are weak. He helps us to learn and grow in Him, in whom we are complete. God wants us to let that love flow to us and through us, so we can be a blessing wherever we go and whatever we do. God wants us as mature faith-filled believers to represent Him well in a crazy world. To walk with God in love, joy and peace is an amazing walk. Those who have a hard heart towards God, God will give him a new heart.

> EZEKIEL 11:19
>
> And I will give them one heart and I will put a spirit within you, and I will take the stony heart out of their flesh and will give them an heart of flesh.
>
> EZEKIEL 36:26-27
>
> A new heart also will I give to you and a new spirit will I put within you, and I will take away the stony heart out of your flesh and I will give you a heart of flesh.

And I will put My Spirit within you and cause you to walk in my statues (God's word), and ye shall keep my judgments and do them.

How amazing is that? A new heart and God's Spirit in us! God in Christ is in us in the Holy Spirit. Walk in Joy, Peace, and God's love. That is what it feels like walking with God.

## August 3, 1999

Time it has passed quickly, right before my eyes.
I find myself gazing up at the beautiful blue sky.
Looking at the trees with their leaves and the bright yellow sun.
Feeling the peacefulness of the forest and just having fun.
Walking through the woods as the squirrels scurry on by.
The breeze feels cool and soft, like a natural high.
The beauty of God's creations gently touching me.
There is no other place I prefer to be.
The woods are enchanting, my soul feels free.
My mind and heart are content, as God walks with me.
The sunset is coming upon the forest and pond, not too far.
While pine needles are glistening like tiny stars.
Reflections on the water of the wilderness, caught at a glance.
Feelings of peace I hold, somehow seem to be enhanced.
The sky though sparkling, but the sun has gone down.
Watching the flames, each seeming to have a turn.
Throwing warmth, as a slight chill appears.
Staring at the moon, the whole world shares.
Looks lovely surrounded by stars all around.
Enjoying the quietness, where here I have found.
Praise God, Praise His Holy amazing name.
His Wonderful, Powerful name in the most Holy name of Jesus Christ.

This is an amazing way to live. Love God, walk and live in the Holy Spirit and do good unto others. Walk in joy and peace and God's love through good times and bad. Tribulations will come the Bible tells us that, but it also says be strong in the Lord. Walk in the power of Jesus Christ resurrection that is available to all faith-filled believers.

> PROVERBS 3:13-17
>
> Happy/blessed is the man that findeth wisdom and the man that getteth understanding.
>
> For the merchandise of it (wisdom) is better than the merchandise of silver and the gain thereof than fine gold.
>
> She (wisdom) is more precious than rubies and all things thou canst desire are not to be compared unto her(wisdom).
>
> Length of days is in her (wisdoms) right hand and in her left riches and honor.
>
> Her (wisdom/ the word) ways are ways of pleasantness, and all her paths are peace.

God knows our hearts and loves us and wants us to know His wisdom, the Word of God. We love Him because He first loved us. He wants us to walk in peace and His love representing Him well as we trust Him and do good unto others. We are His chosen ones, and he wants us to let others see our walk in hope and believing so they will want what we have. They see us believing and trusting God and walking in peace even in the storms of life. Because we know He will fight our battles. We just need to Stand, thank Him and Praise Him.

Paul learnt through his walk with God how to be content and how to be abased. He had trials and tribulations. He spent time in a nasty awful prison and God gave him revelation to write the epistles. His experience with God and His word and the trials and tribulations he suffered, one day at a time with God's help.

He was content and he was an awesome disciple and servant of God. God taught Paul much as he seeked Him and His love and His truth.

> PHILIPPIANS 2:4-5
>
> Look not every man on his own things, but every man also on <u>the things of others.</u>
>
> Let this Mind be in you, which was also in Christ Jesus.
>
> 1 PETER 1:8-10
>
> Whom having not seen, ye love; in whom though now ye see (him) not, yet believed, ye rejoiced with joy unspeakable and full of glory.
>
> Receiving the end of your faith, the salvation of your soul.
>
> Of which salvation the prophets have inquired and searched diligently, who prophesied of the <u>Grace</u> that should come unto you.

Unlike the apostles who got to know and see Jesus we believe with-out seeing. We believe Jesus Christ died and was resurrected to save us and forgive our sins through the Grace given Him and unto us also. God through Jesus Christ has made the Grace administration or dispensation, available to us. The prophets searched diligently the grace administration, which now has been made available to believers who believe with-out seeing. The prophets of old were searching to know Jesus Christ, but it did not happen in their time. People no longer live under the law administration filled with man's legalism, sacrifices, and a million rules. We have been blessed as faith-filled believers in Christ in the Holy Spirit in joy and peace doing good unto others, because He is good to us.

HEBREWS 13:16

But to do good and to communicate forgot not: for with such sacrifices God is well pleased.

That is what God wants for us, to spend our time and maybe money and whatever we need to do good unto others. That is the sacrifice God requires of us and it is pleasing to Him. Learning and growing in the Grace and knowledge of our Lord Jesus Christ. To Him be the glory now and forever.

EPHESIANS 4:15-16

But, speaking the truth in love, may grow up into Him in all things, which is the head, Christ.

From whom the whole body fitly joined together and compacted by that every joint supplieth, according to the effectual working in the measure of every part, maketh increase of the body unto the edifying of itself in love.

We grow in the knowledge of Him and the body of Christ, the church. We are the church fitly joined together in love. The church is fitly joined together is us, all the faith-filled believers walking with God. Buildings are where the believers meet, but the believers are the true Church of God. True and honest believers walking in love. Walk complete in Him with Faith-filled believing God is our sufficiency in everything. He will give you back double for your former troubles and sufferings for Him and you will walk in peace and joy in Him.

I personally look forward to my daily walk with God praising His Holy name and thanking Him for His faithfulness. I expect good things to happen to me every day, as I walk in faith and trust God will walk with me in everything. The word of God says that God is looking and longing for someone to bless! I say, "here I am Lord", waiting and looking and longing to be blessed by God.

PROVERBS 4:21-23

Let them (words in the word of God) not depart from thine eyes, keep them, in the midst of thine heart.

For they (God's word) are life unto those that find them and health to all their flesh.

Keep thine heart with all diligence; for out of it are the issues of life.

Guard the word in your heart and mind and soul with all diligence. Do not let the enemy ever, for any reason, steal your joy and peace.

# CHAPTER 7

# Joy

God gave His only begotten Son to die for us and suffer for our sins and through the resurrection of our Lord Jesus Christ we have power, peace, and joy. Jesus gave us power and authority over the enemy. God has forgiven us our sins and put them as far as the East is from the West and remembers them no more. If we sin, we repent and thank God for His forgiveness and ask Him to help us change in that area. God is the only one who can change you. You cannot change yourself, you have to let God do it or it is just, works of the flesh. God will help you through the Holy Spirit if you ask Him to. Step by step and day by day. God loves us and will work in us as we walk with Him. God in Christ in us in the Holy Spirit. Continue to walk with God and be led by the Holy Spirit in peace and Joy.

PSALMS 46:10

Be still and know that I am God, I will be exalted among the heathen, I will be exalted in the earth.

PSALMS 16:11

Thou will show me the path of life, in Thy (God's) presence is fulness of joy; at Thy (God's) right hand there are pleasures forever more.

God's desire for us is to walk in peace and joy in His love. The Word say's, the joy of the Lord is my strength. God's word is full of wonderful promises we can walk in and enjoy as we believe and trust God, and do good unto others. We can live in all Jesus died for us to have, so why not? There are so many un-happy miserable, and crabby Christians in the world who do not want to apply the truths of God's word in their lives. If you put a little time in God's word it can be a walk of learning and growing with Him. Do you really want to get to know God and receive His love and blessings?

EPHESIANS 3:19

And to know the love of Christ, which passeth knowledge, that ye might be filled with all the fulness of Him.

PSALMS 62:5

My soul, wait Only upon God, and silently submit to Him; for my hope and expectation are from Him.

There should be no reason for an honest faith-filled believer to be miserable. God sets us free and He will help us and take care of us as we walk with Him. Talk to God throughout your day and thank Him and Praise Him and walk in the power of our Lord Jesus Christ. Peace and joy is not a matter of what is going on around you. But through the leadership of the Holy Spirit having total confidence in God. He will bless you as you walk with Him.

JEREMIAH 29:11

For I (God) know the thoughts that I think toward you, saith the Lord, thoughts of peace and not of evil, to give you an expected end.

God thinks of us all the time. He has counted the hairs on our head. Is He always in your thoughts? Selah, ponder and think on these things. The power of faith filled believing is our key that opens up the door of truth that is in God's word and all the promises God has given us. God in Christ in the Holy Spirit in us! Faith is power. So why wouldn't we walk in peace and joy in Christ?

> MATTHEW 10:1
>
> And when He (Jesus) had called unto His twelve disciples, He (Jesus) gave them power against unclean spirits, to cast them out and to heal all manner of sickness and all manner of disease.

We have God in Christ in us through the Holy Spirit, we have power! We are loaded with power and authority in Christ through the Holy Spirit. Just as the apostles had power and authority we do too. What we need is to learn and walk in it in close fellowship with the Father.

> MATTHEW 10:7-8
>
> And as ye go, preaching, saying, the kingdom of God is at hand, Heal the sick, cleanse the lepers, raise the dead, cast out devils, freely ye have received, freely give.

This is the power we have through the blood of Jesus Christ. He has freely given us that power and He wants us to use it and share it with others. Loving them, healing them, and meeting their needs. We have power through faith-filled believing in Christ Jesus. We need to walk in and operate that power in our lives, while walking in peace and joy in believing the word of God.

> MATTHEW 17:20
>
> And Jesus said unto them, Because of your unbelief: for verily I say unto you, If, ye have faith as a grain of

mustard seed, ye shall say unto this mountain, Remove hence to yonder place; and it shall remove; and nothing shall be impossible unto you.

Now, that is the power of faith/believing, which is available to us, right now, today. Faith-filled believing is the key to open the knowledge of God's word to us. The more we believe and ask God to help us learn and grow spiritually in the knowledge of Him, He will help us.

MATTHEW 21:22

And all things, whatsoever ye shall ask in prayer (talking to God), Believing, ye shall receive.

God is there waiting to help us, teach us and open His word and will to us. Walk in daily fellowship with God and ask Him for the help you need. He is there for you.

1 CORINTHIANS 2:4-5

And my speech and my preaching, was not with enticing words of man's wisdom, but in demonstration of the Spirit and of power.

That your faith should not stand in the wisdom of men, but in the power of God.

Paul is telling us to walk in the power and wisdom of God, not men. Paul knew that God wants a close daily relationship with us. God gave us His word so we would know what we have in Christ. The people in the Old Testament wanted what we have available to us today, but they lived in the law administration not the Grace administration. No more animal blood for sacrifices for sins. Jesus was the last blood sacrifice and now God does not require it anymore. Jesus died and rose again so we can have a personal relationship with God in Christ in us through the Holy Spirit with Peace and Joy.

ROMANS 3:20-25

Therefore, by the deeds of the law there shall no flesh be justified in His sight: for by the law is the knowledge of sin.

But now the righteousness of God without the law is manifested, being witnessed by the law and the prophets.

Even the righteousness of God, which is by faith of Jesus Christ unto all and upon all them that believe: for there is no difference.

For all have sinned and come short of the glory of God.

Being justified freely by His grace through the redemption that is in Christ Jesus.

Whom God hath sent forth to be a propitiation payment.

Through faith in His blood, to declare His righteousness for the remission of sins that are passed, through the forbearance of God.

That is what we have through faith-filled believing in our Lord Jesus Christ. We have forgiveness of sins and God's Grace walking with Him in love. If you mess up, repent, receive God's forgiveness and keep moving forward in His love and thank Him and Praise Him. There is NO condemnation for sins or messing up if you are in Christ Jesus. We are made righteous (in right standing with God), and we are justified (made as if we never sinned). We can walk in Jesus Christ through the Holy Spirit in peace and joy walking in God's will and purposes. We can have a joyful, peaceful, abundant life in Christ Jesus.

EPHESIANS 3:20

Now unto Him (God) that is able, to do exceedingly abundantly above all that we ask or think according to the power that worketh in US.

3 JOHN 2

Beloved I wish above all things that thou mayest prosper and be in Health, even as thy soul prospereth.

This is all ours today. God does exceedingly abundantly above all we ask or think. He wants us to prosper and be in Health. Ask for all the best gifts in the spiritual realm and walk with God in peace and joy and your carnal life will also be blessed. No wonder the people in the Old Testament searched the scriptures daily. They were hoping and searching for Jesus Christ and His birth. They studied the word because they wanted and hoped to be part of the grace administration. The birth of Jesus Christ and His resurrection unfortunately, was kept hidden. The mystery of the Grace administration to the believers.

EPHESIANS 3: 3-21

How that by revelation He (God) made know unto me (Paul) the mystery; (as I wrote afore in few words),

Whereby, when ye read, ye may understand my knowledge in the mystery of Christ.

Which in other ages was not made known unto the sons of men, as it is Now Revealed unto His holy apostles and prophets by the Spirit.

That the Gentiles should be fellow-heirs and of the same body and partakers of His promise in Christ by the gospel:

Wherefore I was made a minister, according to the gift of the Grace of God given unto me by the effectual working of His Power.

Unto me (Paul), who am less than the least of all saints, is this grace given, that I should preach among the Gentiles the unsearchable riches of Christ;

And to make all men see what is the fellowship of the mystery, which from the beginning of the world hath been hid in God, who created all things.

To the intent that now unto the principalities and powers in heavenly places might be known by the church the <u>manifold wisdom of God,</u>

According to the eternal purpose which He purposed in Christ Jesus our Lord:

In whom we have boldness and access with <u>confidence by the faith of Him (Jesus).</u>

Wherefore I (Paul) desire that ye faint not at my tribulation for you, which is your glory.

For this cause, I bow my knees unto the Father of our Lord Jesus Christ,

Of whom the whole family in heaven and earth is named,

That He (God) would grant you according to the riches of His glory, to be strengthened with might by His Spirit in the inner man,

That Christ may dwell in your hearts by faith, that ye, being rooted and grounded in love,

May be able to comprehend with all saints (believers) what is the breadth, and the length, and the depth and the height;

And to know the love of Christ, which passeth knowledge, that ye might be Filled with all the fulness of God.

Now unto Him that is able to do exceedingly abundantly above all that we ask or think, according to the power that worketh in us.

Unto Him be glory in the church by Christ Jesus throughout all ages, world without end. Amen.

That is the great mystery that was hid throughout the ages. The mystery had to be hidden because if Satan knew what God's plan was the enemy would not have killed Jesus. But, through the blood of Christ we now have remission of sins and the great gift of Grace. We are saved through Grace through Jesus Christ and we are fellow heirs with Him and partakers of God's promise in Christ. Through Jesus' resurrection we are fully equipped in the fulness of God! That is the manifold wisdom of God. To fill us with the riches of His glory. God wants us to comprehend and understand the breadeth, length, width and height of the love of God in Christ, which passeth carnal knowledge. Knowing the word of God is where you can learn and comprehend and understand, God in Christ in us through the Holy Spirit. Then, you learn how to practically apply the word of God in your daily walk with Him. God's word says He can do exceeding, abundantly above all we ask or think according to the power that works in us. The power of Christ. So, tell me, why are you not filled to overflowing with Peace and Joy in the Holy Spirit? God has blessed us with amazing spiritual blessings in heavenly places. He supplies all our needs as we walk and talk with Him throughout our day.

COLOSSIANS 1:26-29

> Even the mystery, which hath been hid from the ages and from generations, but now is made manifest to all His saints (believers),
>
> To whom God would make known what is the riches of His glory of this mystery among the Gentiles; which is Christ in you the hope of glory.
>
> Whom we preach, warning every man in all wisdom; that we may present every man perfect in Christ Jesus:
>
> Where unto I also labor, striving according to His working, which worketh in me mightily.

God hid the Great Mystery, God in Christ in us in the Holy Spirit, but has made it known unto us. Paul warns and teaches us to walk in all wisdom, the wisdom of God in joy and strength in the Lord. God knows we are not perfect in and of ourselves, but we are complete in God in Christ in us in the Holy Spirit. That makes us perfect in Christ through the Holy Spirit. Jesus Christ suffered and died so that we might have life and have it in abundance.

1 CORINTHIANS 2:7-10

> But we speak the wisdom of God in a mystery (when we speak/pray in tongues), even the hidden wisdom, which God ordained before the world unto our glory.
>
> Which none of the princes of this world (devil spirits) knew: for had they known it, they would not have crucified the Lord of glory.

> But as it is written, eye hath not seen, nor ear heard, neither have entered into the heart of man, the things which God hath prepared for them that love Him.
>
> But God has revealed them unto us by His Spirit: For the Spirit searchest all things, yea, the deep things of God.

The only way to know the deep things of God is to know God's word and ask Him to open the heart of your understanding. God will reveal many things to you if you ask Him. His Spirit will talk to your spirit and lead you, guide you, and teach you. God had to hide the great mystery from the enemy. God in Christ in you in the Holy Spirit. If the enemy knew God's plan for our salvation it would have messed everything up. That is why He had to hide it. God is so amazing, and He loves us and wants us to walk in peace and joy.

### 1 CORINTHIANS 4:1-2

> Let a man so account of us, as of the mystery of Christ and stewards of the mystery of God. Moreover, it is required in stewards, that a man be found faithful.

Yes, as God's faithful believers we are required to be good stewards of God's word. Yes, good and faith-filled representatives of our Lord Jesus Christ. We should be found faithful in Christ in peace and joy. Know God's word and who you are in Christ and stay in peace and joy. Keep believing and trusting God and talking to Him with confidence He will do what His word says He will do. Remember, you are complete in Him.

### PHILIPPIANS 4:6

> Be careful for nothing; but in everything by prayer and supplication with thanksgiving let your requests be made known unto God.

God wants fellowship with you. He wants to talk with you and be with you through your day to day life. He wants us to have a humble and thankful heart and make our request known unto Him. We should always give God thanks and praise for always being there for us.

PHILIPPIANS 4:13

I can do all things through Christ which strengthens me.

As we walk out in the world being fully equipped with all that Jesus died for us to have we can be strengthened and lights in a dark and perverse world. But we have to walk in the Spirit.

ROMANS 8:8-11

So, then they that are in the flesh cannot please God.

But ye are not in the flesh, but in the Spirit, if so be that the Spirit of God dwell in you. Now if any man have not the Spirit of Christ, he is none of us.

And if Christ be in you, the body is dead because of sin; but the Spirit is life because of righteousness.

But, if the Spirit of Him that raised up Jesus from the dead dwell in you, He that raised up Christ from the dead shall also quicken your mortal bodies by His Spirit that dwelleth in you.

We are, God in Christ in us through the Holy Spirit and the righteousness we have in Christ. Let the Holy Spirit work with your spirit and teach you and love you. Truly walk with God daily and He will walk with you and bless you.

JOEL 2:26

And ye shall eat in plenty and be satisfied and praise the name of the Lord your God, that has dealt wondrously with you: and My people shall never be ashamed.

PSALMS 147:14

He maketh peace in thy borders …..

ISAIAH 54:10

For the mountains shall depart and the hills be removed: but My kindness shall not depart from thee, neither shall the covenant of My peace be moved saith the Lord that hath mercy on thee.

All these promises and all those in God's word are for us. Peace is in your daily walk with God through your godly behavior and you will stay in joy. When things get tough and your struggling, talk to God and cast your care on Him and ask Him to help you get back to peace and walk you through it. Thank Him for all He has blessed you with. God works things out for good to those who are in Christ Jesus. All things are possible with God to those who love Him and are called to His purposes.

ROMANS 8:32-39

He that spared not His own Son, but delivered Him up for us all, how shall He not with him also freely give us all things?

Who shall lay anything to the charge of God's elect? It is God that justifieth.

> Who is he that condemneth? It is Christ that died, yea rather, that is risen again, who is even at the right hand of God, who also maketh intercession for us.
>
> Who shall separate us from the love of Christ? Shall tribulation or distress or persecution or famine or nakedness or peril or sword?
>
> As it is written, For thy sake we are killed all the day long; we are counted as sheep for the slaughter.
>
> Nay, in all these things we are more than conquers through Him that loved us.
>
> For I am persuaded, that neither death nor life nor angels nor principalities nor things present or things to come,
>
> Nor height nor depth nor any other creature, shall be able to separate us from the love of God, which is in Christ Jesus our Lord.

As we walk daily with God and talk to Him and study His word we learn as committed faith-filled believers trusting God through Christ in us through the Holy Spirit. Then we will not let anything separate us from the love of God. God loves us! We diligently strive to walk in His love and protect His word in our hearts, in everything we do. He is always looking and longing for someone to bless.

What is your walk with God like?

Do you spend time on a regular basis with God and in His word?

Do you seek God daily and talk to Him?

Do you ask Him to be involved in every part of your life?

Do you thank God daily for loving you and taking care of you?

Do you believe in the hope of Jesus Christ?

Do you believe you can walk in peace and joy?

Do you trust God with faith-filled love and believing?

Do you believe God is able to do what His word says He can do?

Do you believe all things are possible with God to all those who love Him and are called to His purposes?

Do you believe you are complete in Him?

Do you believe, God in Christ in you through the Holy Spirit?

> ROMANS 5:5
>
> And hope maketh not ashamed; because the love of God is shed abroad in our hearts by the Holy Spirit which is given unto us.
>
> ROMANS 12:11
>
> Not slothful in business (all parts of your life); fervent in spirit; serving the Lord.
>
> ROMANS 15:13
>
> Now the God of hope fill you with all joy and peace in believing, that ye may abound in hope through the power of the Holy Spirit.

God in Christ in us through the Holy Spirit. Enjoy all that Jesus died for us to have and walk in peace and joy. Walk in the grace of God and let the Holy Spirit guide you and help you in your walk.

EPHESIANS 4:7-8

> But unto everyone of us is given grace according to the measure of the gift of Christ.
>
> Wherefore, He saith, when He (Jesus) ascended upon high, He led captivity captive and gave gifts unto men.

We are saved through the Grace of God who has given all believers that wonderful gift of grace. We should let that grace flow through us and to others representing God well.

# CHAPTER 8

# God In Christ In Us Through The Holy Spirit

We have power through the grace of God. We walk in His love and have all that Jesus is. God has given us so much strength, love, peace, and joy. He has given us so much to be thankful for. He has made us complete in Him.

> EPHESIANS 1:7
>
> In whom (Jesus Christ) we have redemption through His blood, the forgiveness (remission) of sins, according to the riches of His (God's) grace.
>
> EPHESIANS 2:8-9
>
> For by grace (gift of God) are you saved through faith and that not of yourselves: it is the gift of God.
>
> Not of works, least any man should boast.

Through God's grace we have power in the name of Jesus Christ. Jesus died to set us free from sin and the law and condemnation and doubt, worry and fear. A life free from confusion. There is so much more that we have through Christ. The list goes on and on. I will try to show you through the word all we have available through God and our Lord Jesus Christ.

MATTHEW 9:6-8

But that ye may know that the Son of man hath power on earth to forgive sins, (then sayest He to the sick of palsy,) arise, take up thy bed and go unto thine house.

And he arose and departed to his house.

But when the multitude saw it, they marveled and glorified God, which had given such power unto men.

And as Jesus passed forth from thence, he saw a man, named Matthew, sitting at the receipt of custom: and He sayest unto him, Follow me. And he arose and followed Him.

Jesus gave power to all of us, even power to defeat the enemy. We can walk as He would have us, walking in His will and purposes. Believing with faith-filled believing with praise and thankfulness to God in the name of Jesus Christ. Even in tough times we can still be stable because we trust God. Believing and trusting God enables us to walk in stability, peace, joy and total confidence in God in all things.

ROMANS 16:25-27

Now to Him that is of power to stablish you according to My gospel and the preaching of Jesus Christ, according to the revelation of the mystery, which was kept secret since the world began,

But now is made manifest and by the scriptures of the prophets according to the commandment of the everlasting God, made known to all nations for the obedience of faith.

To God only wise, be glory through Jesus Christ forever. Amen.

When I read these scriptures and believe them with Faith, I see tremendous power through Jesus Christ to us. Let the Holy Spirit fill you to overflowing with power and grace and mercy and forgiveness and love others. We are able through the Holy Spirit to do all that God wants us to do.

We need not to get hurt or angry or offended, we are mature faith-filled believers walking in the love of Christ, so let us act like it. The word of God tells us numerous times to love and bless our enemies. Not for them, but for us, so we can stay and walk in peace and then we will be blessed.

LUKE 6:35-38

But love your enemies and do good and lend, hoping for nothing again and your reward shall be great and ye shall be the children of the Highest: for He is kind unto the unthankful and to the evil.

Be ye therefore merciful, as your Father also is merciful.

Judge not and ye shall not be judged; condemn not and ye shall not be condemned; forgive and ye shall be forgiven.

Give and it shall be given unto you; good measure pressed down and shaken together and running over shall men give unto your bosom. For with the same measure that ye measure withal it shall be measured to you again.

God wants us to stay in peace and joy and He wants to bless us. But that will not happen if you have unforgiveness in your heart. If we forgive our enemies and pray for them and bless them God will bless us for walking in His will. The word of God does not tell us we have to feel like it, but it does tell us to do it. If we stay in peace and joy and forgive our enemies God will bless us for walking in His word.

MATTHEW 5:44

But I (Jesus) say unto you, love your enemies, bless them that curse you, do good to them that hate you and pray for them which despitefully use you and persecute you.

It takes time and practice and a lot of studying the word of God to be able to forgive, pray and bless your enemies. But once you learn to walk in God's will your reward shall be great. It will with time get easier and easier, as you trust God. It is true, God will bless you for walking in His word with believing and trust in Him and His mighty power. He will open the doors of your understanding and knowledge of Him. By God's grace we can do all things through Christ who is our strength. God has through His grace fully prepared us to walk in His will and purposes in Christ through the Holy Spirit.

CORINTHIANS 15: 10

But by the grace of God, I (Paul) am what I am and His grace which was bestowed upon me was not in vain: but I laboured (studied) more abundantly than they all: yet not I but the grace of God which was within me.

God in Christ in us through the Holy Spirit. Praise God! Faith filled believers can walk in the confidence of knowing God will never leave us. God will help us and take care of us as we walk in His rest and the peace of Jesus Christ.

> MATTHEW 11:28-30
>
> Come unto Me all ye that labour and are heavy laden and I will give you rest.
>
> Take My yoke upon you and learn of Me: for I am meek and lowly in heart: and ye shall find rest for your souls.
>
> For My yoke is easy and My burden is light.
>
> JOHN 16:33
>
> These things I (Jesus) have spoken unto you. That in Me ye might have peace. In the world ye shall have tribulation: but be of good cheer; I (Jesus) have overcome the world.

How refreshing is that? Jesus has overcome the world/enemy. So, we can walk in peace. Jesus died and rose again so we could live and enjoy all that He died for us to have in abundance. (John 10:10) God in Christ in us through the Holy Spirit in peace, joy and power in abundance.

> ACTS 2:38-39
>
> Then Peter said unto them, repent and be baptized every one of you in the name of Jesus Christ for the remission of sins, and ye shall receive the gift of the Holy Ghost (Spirit).
>
> For the promise is unto you and to your children and to all that are a far off, even as many as the Lord our God shall call.

For the promise is unto you and to your children and to all that are a far off, even as many as the Lord your God shall call. What a promise.

> Acts 4:33
>
> And with great power gave the apostles witness of the Lord Jesus Christ: and great grace was upon them all.
>
> ACTS 10:38
>
> How God appointed Jesus of Nazareth with the Holy Spirit and with power, who (Jesus) went about doing good and healing all the were oppressed of the devil: for God was with Him(Jesus).

Jesus went about doing good. He healed people and delivered those oppressed of the devil and helped people where ever He went. Jesus always took time to pray and talk to God through out His day. Jesus walked in complete fellowship with the Father and we can have that too. God in Christ in us through the Holy Spirit is what our walk should be. That is complete faith filled fellowship with God.

BOSTON CHILDRENS HOSPITAL          4/13/1992

We left at 8:15AM we were on our way.
Quite a ride, quite a long day
Finally, we are there, the wind is blowing.
Walking quickly, glad it is not snowing.
Now we are warm, here is the direction we're going.
Being early, a little detour we took to pass the time.
I went first, the others waited, it was fine.
That tiny prick gets ya just a little
Kids lives depend on it, so do not diddle.
Every drop counts in a serious emergency.
After donating blood we were late of course.
We had to wait for a while, but no remorse.

Once we went in the report was good.
Doc said everything looks well, as it should.
See you back here in six months from now.
Next time we will go to our appointment on time, Wow.

Thank you, Holy Father, in the name of Jesus Christ through the Holy Spirit for loving us and taking care of us. You are so wonderful and truly amazing.

God will help us to and through anything through His Grace and Mercy. I can't say enough about how important it is to walk and talk with God throughout our day. Walk in the power of our Lord Jesus Christ in His love and God's word. God will work things out for our good, even if they are not so good right now. Trust and have confidence in God that all things are possible to those who love Him and are called to His purposes.

> ROMANS 14:17-19
>
> For the kingdom of God is not meat and drink, but righteousness, peace and joy in the Holy Spirit.
>
> For he that in these things serveth Christ is acceptable to God and approved of men.
>
> Let us therefore, follow after things which make for peace and things wherewith one may edify another.

We are to walk in God's will in peace and follow the leading of the Holy Spirit, while He watches over you in God's love. Keep God's word in your heart at all times, it is the sword of the Spirit.

> PROVERBS 4:23
>
> Keep thy heart with all diligence; for out of it are the issues of life.

There is one way to know God and that way is through knowing His word. God wants us to know Him, as He knows us. God wants us to learn His Character, His will and His ways. If we walk in His ways and in His word, God blesses us because we are committed to Him. God sees our walk and I pray it is pleasing to Him. God's word is where we learn about close fellowship with our Holy Almighty Father. As your understanding grows you grow in the knowledge of God. Learn what Jesus' death, resurrection and ascension into heaven means for your life. Learn who you are in Christ Jesus and walk in the power we have through Him. Learn how important this is for a faith filled believers' life.

2 TIMOTHY 2:15

Study to show thyself approved unto God, a workman (of God's word) that needeth not to be ashamed, rightly dividing the word of truth.

1 THESSALONIANS 5:21-24

Prove all things (by studying God's word) hold fast that which is good.

Abstain from all appearance of evil (be godly representatives of Jesus Christ in us).

And the very God of peace sanctify you wholly and I pray God your whole spirit and soul and body be preserved blameless unto the coming of our Lord Jesus Christ.

Faithful is He (God) that calleth you, Who also will do it.

1 THESSALONIANS 4:11

And that ye study to be quiet and to do your own business (mind your own business) and to work with your own hands, as we commanded you.

JUDE 20-21

But ye, beloved, building up yourselves on your most holy faith, praying in the Holy Spirit.

Keep yourselves in the love of God in his mercy through our Lord Jesus Christ unto eternal life.

JOHN 5:39

Search (study) the scriptures for in them ye think ye have eternal life: and they are they which testify (walk with God) of Me.

Again, the only way to know God and learn to walk with Him is to study and learn God's word. As we put time in God's word and ask Him to open the heart of our understanding, He will show you amazing things. God helps us right where we are at and we learn and grow from there.

Other scriptures you can look at: study God's word.

1 TIMOTHY 3:15

ACTS 17:11

PROVERBS 15:28

God by revelation gave His word to the apostle Paul to be written down, so we can learn and grow in Him. The word of God is God breathed.

2 TIMOTHY 3:16

> All scripture is given by inspiration of God and is profitable for doctrine, for reproof, for correction, for instruction in righteousness.

God in Christ in us through the Holy Spirit. God's word is profitable and we should learn from the doctrine, reproof and correction in righteousness. God's Spirit teaches our spirit and our spirit teaches our mind and our soul, then they work together and we can walk in fellowship with our Holy Father. Trust God and do good unto others, as His workman that needeth not to be ashamed. We are called the saints, the believers in Christ. When Stephen was being stoned to death, he pray for those stoning him and asked God not to hold it against them.

ACTS 7:60

> And he (Stephen) kneeled down and cried with a loud voice, Lord, lay not this sin to their charge. And when he had said this, he fell asleep (died).

> If Stephen prayed for those who killed him, we should pay attention. Pray for those who hurt you and bless them. Jesus prayed for those who crucified Him. Jesus, our example of how to walk with God. Jesus prayed to the Father for His murderers.

LUKE 23:34

> Then said Jesus, Father, forgive them for they know not what they do. And they parted His garment and casts lots.

We have Jesus praying for those who killed Him. That is great power, praying for those who hurt us. Satan does not even know what to do with that. We should follow in the ways of Jesus Christ.

1 PETER 2:21

For hereunto were ye called because Christ also suffered for us, leaving us an example, that ye should follow His steps.

MATTHEW 5:44

But I (Jesus) say unto you, Love your enemies, bless them that curse you, do good to them that hate you and pray for them which despitefully use you and persecute you.

That sounds so difficult and tough to do. To forgive and pray and bless those who truly hurt you. But, look at Stephen and Paul and Jesus, they prayed for those who beat them and killed them. 1 Peter 2:21, says we are to follow Jesus' example. Forgiving and praying and blessing those who do us wrong opens a door of tremendous power and blessings in our lives. Remember, this is not our permanent residence, we have a mansion in the sky, we are just passing through helping Jesus.

JOHN 4:1-3

Let not your heart be troubled, ye believe in God, believe also in Me (Jesus).

In My Fathers house are many mansions, if it were not so I would have told you. I go to prepare a place for you.

And if I go and prepare a place for you, I will come again and receive you unto Myself, that where I am, there you may be also.

Walking with God and trusting Him completely will help you forgive others and pray for them and bless them. Only then can you stay in perfect peace and be blessed. It shows you honor God's word and the truths therein. Seek God daily and ask Him to Help you grow in all His word. Ask and keep on asking and it shall be given you.

According to God's word. If you are struggling in a certain area, ask of the giving God. Know that you have power and authority in Jesus Christ (Luke 4:32).

YOU HAVE POWER
In the gift of Grace
In the faith of Jesus Christ (1 Corinthians 2:4)
In Believing (Matt. 22:21-22, Luke 8:5)
In Joy (Romans 14:22, Matt. 25:21)
In Peace (Matt. 11:28-31)
In Forgiveness (2 Corinthians 2:9-10)
In the Holy Spirit (Acts 1:8)
In the gifts of the Spirit (Galatians 5:22-23)
In Wisdom (Matt. 13:44)
In praying for your enemies (Matt 5:44-48)
In wisdom and the word of God and true fellowship with Him.
In Hope
In Praying
In Thanksgiving and Praise
In Mercy
In God's Love

God wants our love, as He freely gives us His love. We love Him because He first loved us. God strengthens us and upholds us in our daily walk with Him.

> ISAIAH 41:10
>
> Fear thou not; for I am with thee; be not dismayed; for I am thy God: I will strengthen thee: yea, I will uphold thee with the right hand of My righteousness.

God is always there strengthening us and literally taking care of us each and every second of every day. God will walk and talk with us in our daily ups and downs. I talk to God throughout my day about everything. I ask for His help and guidance in all I do. I ask God to guide me by His Spirit, so I can walk in His will and heart for me. I believe and trust God with faith filled believing that He is working in my life, even if I don't see it right now.

COLOSSIANS 3:23-23

And whatsoever you do, do it heartily, as to the Lord and not unto men;

Knowing that of the Lord ye shall receive the reward of the inheritance: for ye serve the Lord Christ.

Acknowledge God daily, study His word, talk to Him and be thankful and praise Him,

His word, talk to Him and be thankful and praise Him, all the day long.

ISAIAH 40:31

But they that wait upon the Lord shall renew their strength; they shall mount up with wings as eagles; they shall run and not be weary and they shall walk and faint not.

God's arms are always open to hold us up, helping us through the good times and bad. Walk with Him daily it is that important. The word of God is filled with treasures to be searched out by us, God's faith filled believers. We are to be God's examples and representatives. Wherever we go we are God's examples in a crazy mixed up world. God wants people to see God in Christ in us through the Holy Spirit. God wants people to want what we have. Walk in God's character in our actions and the words we use and our behavior. How else will they want what we have?

### PHILIPPIANS 4:11-13

Not that I speak in respect of want: for I have learned in whatsoever state I am, therewith to be content.

I know both how to be abased and how to abound: everywhere and in all things, I am instructed both to be full and to be hungry, both to abound and to suffer need.

I can do all things through Christ which strengthens me.

Paul is telling us to be stable in whatever situation we are in. To walk in peace and be content. Christ strengthens us no matter the circumstances in our lives. Trust God, do good unto others, even your enemies and you will please God and He will be with you. You are complete in Him. God can turn around any situation in our lives for our good. Put your faith and trust in God who is able to do exceedingly abundantly above all we ask or think. Be who God wants you to be, a spiritually mature faith filled follower and believer of our Lord Jesus Christ.

### JAMES 1:2-5

My brethren, count it all joy when ye fall into divers temptations;

Knowing this, that the trying of your faith worketh patience.

But let patience have her perfect work, that ye may be perfect and entire, wanting for nothing.

> If any of you lack wisdom let him ask of God, that giveth to all men liberally and up-braideth not and it shall be given him.

God wants nothing more than to help us learn and grow in the knowledge of Him. Grow spiritually and walk in peace. If we lack wisdom or knowledge, ask God who gives liberally. Grow in His love. God will open your heart with understanding, wisdom and knowledge.

ROMANS 5:3-5

> And not only so, but we glory in tribulations also; knowing that tribulation worketh patience;

> And patience, experience, and experience, hope:

> And hope maketh not ashamed; because the love of God is shed abroad in our hearts by the Holy Spirit which is given unto us.

God in Christ in us in the Holy Spirit. Walk ye in it through the love of God in Christ in us. Talk to God through out your day and be thankful and praise His Holy name. Getting to know God is an amazing walk to enjoy. Know God's word and search it daily and learn His character and show that to the world, that is why we are here. Be God's examples walking in His will and represent Him well.

PROVERBS 16:24

> Pleasant words are as an honeycomb, sweet to the soul and health to the bones.

PSALMS 39:7

> And now Lord, what wait I for? My hope is in Thee.

Learn and grow and develop your relationship with God by the leading of the Holy Spirit. Let your behavior and your words be pleasing to God. The Lords correction and reproof is to help us grow and because He loves us. My hope, my peace, my joy, my strength and my heart are in the Lord. Claim all God's promises He has given to us in His word. We are complete in Him, as we believe His word and walk in His will.

ROMANS 15:13

Now the God of hope fill you with all joy and peace in believing, that ye may abound in hope, through the <u>power</u> of the Holy Spirit.

We will abound in hope and overflow with confidence in His promises. When you talk with God ask Him to help you in all you do. Expect God to be good to you everyday and to help you help others along your way. God wants us to be a help and a blessing to others as, His chosen ones.

GALATIANS 6:9 KJV

Let us not grow weary in well doing: for in due season we shall reap, if you faint not.

GALATIANS 6:9 NIV

Let us not grow weary or become discouraged in doing good, for at the proper time we will reap, if we do not give in (to the devil's devices).

PSALMS 139:1

O Lord, Thou hast searched me and known me.

God knows us and He knows our heart for Him and His word and His son Jesus Christ. God is the Alpha and the Omega the beginning and the end. Walk with God in joy and peace and fellowship.

ISAIAH 26:3

> Thou will keep him in perfect peace, whose mind is stayed on Thee: because he trusteth in Thee.

Trusting God gives us peace. God says He will keep us in perfect peace if our minds are stayed on Him. If God gives you the opportunity to help someone, do it in peace because it is a great opportunity to show God's love to others. Forgive, pray and bless your enemies and God will take care of us. He will bless you according to His promises. God is not a respecter of persons. God does not lie. He is faithful to His Holy word.

COLOSSIANS 3:25

> For he that doeth wrong shall receive for the wrong which he hath done: and there is no respecter of persons.

Be strong in the Lord and in the power of His might. Trust in His faithfulness and mercy and grace and forgiveness and the gifts and promises God has bestowed unto us.

EPHESIANS 1:17-23

> That the God of our Lord Jesus Christ, the Father of glory, may give unto you the spirit of wisdom and revelation in the knowledge of Him:

> The eyes of your understanding being enlightened; that ye may know what is the hope of His calling and what the riches of His glory of His inheritance in the saints.

And what is the exceeding greatness of His power to us-ward who believe, according to the working of His mighty power.

Which He wrought in Christ, when He raised Him from the dead and set Him at His own right hand in heavenly places.

Far above all principalities and power and dominion and every name that is named, not only in this world, but also in that which is to come:

And hath put all things under His feet and gave Him to be head over all things to the church,

Which is His body, the fulness of Him that filleth all in all.

# CONCLUSION

I am hoping and believing this book has helped you grow deeper in the word of God and in fellowship with Him. I pray you have a faith filled life, being stable at all times. There is so much more I would like to share with you, but another time. It has been a joy and a privilege to share what God has taught me over the years.

I pray you spend time daily in God's word and ask Him to open His word up to you. Ask God to help you learn what He wants you to and grow in Him. Be a person who strives to walk in the presence of God in good times and bad. Let your behavior be acceptable to God with your actions, words, and how you behave. Not reacting to situations that arises, step back and talk to God Asking Him to help you. Stay in the power of peace, which He has already given us. When situations pop up and they do remember, God in Christ in us in the Holy Spirit working in your spirit helping you through. Praise God and thank Him for His faithfulness, for taking care of us and for fully equipping us to be who God wants us to be. We are complete in Him, through the blood of Jesus Christ.

God has given us His son, Jesus Christ, His love, the Holy Spirit, grace, mercy, forgiveness, the gifts of the Holy Spirit and has revealed the Great Mystery to us.

Learning and studying God's word and walking and talking with Him daily is the very best thing we can do for our lives. Walking in peacefulness and stability and joy is a wonderful amazing life. Faith filled believing with confidence in God knowing in your heart of hearts, God loves us. He will do all His word says He will do. Be examples in a crazy mixed up world. Show others who you are in Christ.

www.ingramcontent.com/pod-product-compliance
Lightning Source LLC
LaVergne TN
LVHW042248070526
838201LV00089B/67